beds & borders

beds & borders

simple projects for
the weekend gardener

Richard Bird

photography by Stephen Robson

RYLAND
PETERS
& SMALL

LONDON NEW YORK

For this edition:

Senior designer *Sally Powell*

Senior editor *Clare Double*

Production *Sheila Smith*

Art director *Gabriella Le Grazie*

Publishing director *Alison Starling*

Illustrators *Martine Collings, Tracy Fennell, Valerie Hill, Stephen Hird, Sarah Kensington, Amanda Patton, Elizabeth Pepperell, Lizzie Sanders, Helen Smythe, Ann Winterbotham*

First published in the United Kingdom in 1998
and reissued with amendments in 2005
by Ryland Peters & Small
20–21 Jockey's Fields
London WC1R 4BW
www.rylandpeters.com

10 9 8 7 6 5 4 3 2 1

ISBN 1 84172 805 5

A CIP record for this book is available from the
British Library.

Printed and bound in China.

contents

introduction

The use of borders is the very essence of gardening. They are a means of producing a pleasant environment that is a joy to be in. They can excite or soothe depending on the mood created, they can be filled with colour or they can present a mantle of foliage. Beds and borders can appeal to all the senses; the sense of smell, of course, and sound – why not plant a bed especially to enjoy the soothing rustle of leaves, grasses and bamboos, easing the mind; and even taste, as many flowers are edible. Borders are the backdrop against which you can relax and enjoy the pleasures of an outside space.

The projects in this book cover a broad range of borders that can be created using a wide variety of plants. Most can be modified for any size of garden, from a small courtyard to a number of acres. Adaptability is the key. While you are at liberty to copy faithfully what is described, you are encouraged to experiment and extend your own experience. Add or substitute plants that you like or whose colours you prefer. Use this book as a jumping-off point, and with patience your efforts will be amply rewarded.

Richard Bird

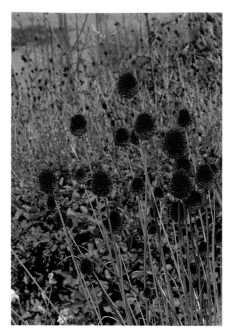  

traditional borders

take many forms and can be adapted at will to suit a garden. Annuals bring a flash of colour or subtler hues and are ideal for graphic planting schemes; single colours bring harmony; while the classic herbaceous border cannot be matched for the impression of abundance and variety it lends to a garden. Borders and beds are important focal points, so they should be planned and tended with care.

above left Formality is not always wanted. Here, cottage-style charm is given by *Allium schoenoprasum,* or chives.

above centre Mixed borders allow a pleasing variety of shapes and forms: scabious and salvia mingle with roses.

above right Always consider how flower forms will combine as well as colours. A cluster of star shapes looks cheerful.

centre right A well-conceived border will give colour, height, variety and a clear mood to a garden. It will add inspiring forefront focus or clear background interest to a view.

right Fill upright spaces so that the eye is led through the scheme, as here: low-growing edging plants are linked by the mid-height lilies to a prominent, honeysuckle-clad rose. The space is well filled without appearing congested.

above Foliage is there to be used in its own right as well as making a fine foil to bold blooms. It affords a wealth of shapes, textures and colours, as well as permanence with evergreen displays.

below Plants have a way of softening edges and blending. Fanning phlox, foxgloves and alliums weave towards dark aquilegia.

above A harmonious colour scheme in a border can be enhanced by using a similar palette beyond the border. An expanse of verbascum is coupled with the beautiful champagne rose 'Graham Thomas' and a fine tower of *Rosa* 'Frau Karl Druschki'.

left Movement and rhythm are at the heart of this interesting foliage scheme, which is punctuated by subtle flower tones.

herbaceous border

Herbaceous borders are back. Having suffered a decline in the earlier part of the twentieth century, interest in herbaceous plants has never been so great. They are versatile, presenting the gardener with a tremendous range of colours, shapes, textures and scents, and in spite of a reputation for being labour-intensive, they take less looking after than many shrubs such as roses. For those who have been wary of using herbaceous plants, a whole new world is there to be explored.

PLANTING SCHEME

Achillea millefolium 'Cerise Queen' (x 5)
Achillea filipendulina 'Gold Plate' (x 6)
Alchemilla mollis (x 3)
Aquilegia 'Crimson Star' (x 9)
Asphodeline lutea (x 5)
Astilbe chinensis var. pumila (x 3)
Eremurus subsp. stenophyllus (x 1)
Euphorbia griffithii 'Fireglow' (x 3)
Helenium autumnale (x 3)

Helianthus 'Loddon Gold' (x 1)
Hemerocallis 'Marion Vaughn' (x 1)
Kniphofia 'Percy's Pride' (x 1)
Lychnis chalcedonica (x 3)
Malva moschata (x 3)
Mimulus 'Royal Velvet' (x 3)
Nectaroscordum siculum (x 12)
Oenothera fruticosa 'Fyreverken' (x 2)
Oenothera stricta (x 2)

Penstemon 'Andenken an Friedrich Hahn' (x 1)
Polemonium pauciflorum (x 4)
Sedum 'Ruby Glow' (x 2)
Solidago cutleri (x 1)
Solidago 'Laurin' (x 1)
Trifolium rubens (x 1)
Verbascum bombyciferum (x 3)

planting scheme

1 *Achillea millefolium* 'Cerise Queen' (x 5)
2 *Achillea filipendulina* 'Gold Plate' (x 6)
3 *Alchemilla mollis* (x 3)
4 *Aquilegia* 'Crimson Star' (x 9)
5 *Asphodeline lutea* (x 5)
6 *Astilbe chinensis* var. *pumila* (x 3)
7 *Eremurus* subsp. *stenophyllus* (x 1)
8 *Euphorbia griffithii* 'Fireglow' (x 3)
9 *Helenium autumnale* (x 3)
10 *Helianthus* 'Loddon Gold' (x 1)
11 *Hemerocallis* 'Marion Vaughn' (x 1)
12 *Kniphofia* 'Percy's Pride' (x 1)
13 *Lychnis chalcedonica* (x 3)

14 *Malva moschata* (x 3)
15 *Mimulus* 'Royal Velvet' (x 3)
16 *Nectaroscordum siculum* (x 12)
17 *Oenothera fruticosa* 'Fyreverken' (x 2)
18 *Oenothera stricta* (x 2)
19 *Penstemon* 'Andenken an Friedrich Hahn' (x 1)
20 *Polemonium pauciflorum* (x 4)
21 *Sedum* 'Ruby Glow' (x 2)
22 *Solidago cutleri* (x 1)
23 *Solidago* 'Laurin' (x 1)
24 *Trifolium rubens* (x 1)
25 *Verbascum bombyciferum* (x 3)

The secret of creating a successful herbaceous border is to make certain that the ground is prepared thoroughly before planting begins. It is essential that all perennial weeds are removed, and generous quantities of well-rotted organic matter should be added as the border will not be dug again for several years. Such preparations are well worth the time and effort involved.

designing

There is no definitive shape for a herbaceous border; it should be designed to fit the space available. However, if possible, the bed should be wide; the ideal is a width of at least twice the height of the tallest plants to be used. This border is 6 x 3.5 m (20 x 12 ft). A backdrop of a green hedge will help to display the flowers to advantage, although an island bed makes a fine focal point. The border should have the tallest flowers at the back and shorter ones towards the front. Plan the arrangement of plants on paper before planting and cater for year-round interest by including plants for each season.

spacing

If you want to create an abundant look quickly, arrange the plants in close proximity. If you can wait, which is better, allow more growing room.

spring underplanting

Herbaceous borders usually come into their own from early summer onwards. Because of the dense growth required to keep a plant in flower right through to the autumn, it is difficult to accommodate spring flowers as well. However, there are a few, bulbs in particular, that can be used as they soon die back and take up little or no space later in the year. Winter-flowering pansies and forget-me-nots can be taken out as the herbaceous growth begins.

alternative planting

1 *Delphinium* hybrids (x 6)

2 *Campanula portenschlagiana* (x 3)

3 *Veronica* 'Shirley Blue' (x 3)

4 *Veronica longifolia* (x 3)

5 *Eryngium alpinum* (x 3)

6 *Geranium* 'Johnson's Blue' (x 1)

7 *Salvia uliginosa* (x 3)

8 *Salvia × sylvestris* 'Blauhügel' (x 1)

9 *Aster × frikartii* 'Mönch' (x 1)

10 *Agapanthus* 'Bressingham Blue' (x 3)

11 *Echinops ritro* (x 1)

12 *Perovskia atriplicifolia* (x 1)

13 *Campanula lactiflora* (x 1)

14 *Aster ericoides* 'Blue Star' (x 1)

15 *Miscanthus sinensis* (x 1)

16 *Salvia sclarea* var. *turkestanica* (x 3)

17 *Bupleurum falcatum* (x 3)

18 *Argyranthemum* 'Jamaica Primrose' (x 3)

19 *Antirrhinum* 'Yellow Triumph' (x 5)

20 *Lilium* 'Limelight' (x 3)

21 *Kniphofia* 'Yellow Hammer' (x 1)

22 *Oenothera stricta* (x 3)

23 *Verbascum bombyciferum* (x 5)

24 *Baptisia australis* (x 1)

25 *Nigella damascena* (x 5)

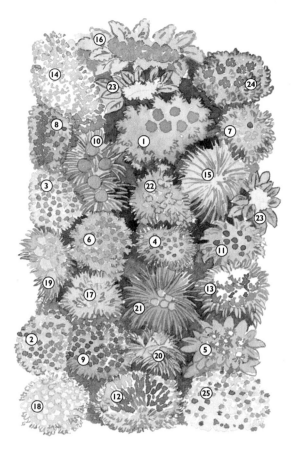

selecting colours

Because herbaceous plants are so diverse, the palette of a bed can be controlled very successfully. This alternative scheme is 'cool' where the main scheme is 'hot'.

care and maintenance

- In autumn, tidy the border, removing dead and dying growth; follow with a mulch.
- Make sure the bed does not become too congested as this can harm and even kill plants.
- Divide vigorous plants regularly, discarding the older sections.

single-colour bed

When visiting gardens, nothing attracts more attention than a border devoted to one colour.
The white garden at Sissinghurst and the red one at Hidcote, two of the finest English
gardens, are famous throughout the world and have been much copied. Even when
inspiration is taken from an exemplary planting, each gardener can make his or her own
choice and arrangement of plants, making a single-colour border very much their own.

PLANTING SCHEME

perennials
Alcea rugosa (x 3)
Anemone hupehensis var.
japonica 'Prinz Heinrich' (x 3)
Aster novi-belgii 'Carnival'
(x 3)
Aster novae-angliae 'Andenken
an Alma Pötschke' (x 3)
Astilbe × arendsii 'Fanal' (x 3)
Centranthus ruber (x 3)
Echinacea purpurea (x 3)
Filipendula rubra (x 5)
Geranium psilostemon (x 1)
Geranium 'Ann Folkard' (x 1)
Lupinus 'The Chatelaine' (x 1)

Lychnis viscaria 'Flore Pleno'
(x 3)
Lythrum virgatum 'The Rocket'
(x 2)
Penstemon 'Evelyn' (x 1)
Penstemon 'Andenken an
Friedrich Hahn' (x 1)
Persicaria affinis (x 3)
Physostegia virginiana 'Red
Beauty' (x 3)
Sanguisorba obtusa (x 3)
Sedum telephium subsp.
maximum 'Atropurpureum'
(x 3)
Sedum spectabile (x 3)

bulbs
Crinum × powellii (x 3)
Dahlia 'Betty Bowen' (x 3)
Schizostylis coccinea (x 5)
Tulipa 'Queen of Night' (x 7)

shrubs
Deutzia × elegantissima (x 1)
Rosa 'Mme Isaac Pereire' (x 1)

annuals
Antirrhinum majus 'His
Excellency' (x 7)
Atriplex hortensis var. *rubra*
(x 5)
Dianthus chinensis 'Firecarpet'
(x 5)
Papaver somniferum (x 3)
Verbena 'Showtime' (x 7)

planting scheme

perennials

1 *Alcea rugosa* (x 3)

2 *Anemone hupehensis* var. *japonica* 'Prinz Heinrich' (x 3)

3 *Aster novi-belgii* 'Carnival' (x 3)

4 *Aster novae-angliae* 'Andenken an Alma Pötschke' (x 3)

5 *Astilbe × arendsii* 'Fanal' (x 3)

6 *Centranthus ruber* (x 3)

7 *Echinacea purpurea* (x 3)

8 *Filipendula rubra* (x 5)

9 *Geranium psilostemon* (x 1)

10 *Geranium* 'Ann Folkard' (x 1)

11 *Lupinus* 'The Chatelaine' (x 1)

12 *Lychnis viscaria* 'Flore Pleno' (x 3)

13 *Lythrum virgatum* 'The Rocket' (x 2)

14 *Penstemon* 'Evelyn' (x 1)

15 *Penstemon* 'Andenken an Friedrich Hahn' (x 1)

16 *Persicaria affinis* (x 3)

17 *Physostegia virginiana* 'Red Beauty' (x 3)

18 *Sanguisorba obtusa* (x 3)

19 *Sedum telephium* subsp. *maximum* 'Atropurpureum' (x 3)

20 *Sedum spectabile* (x 3)

bulbs

21 *Crinum × powellii* (x 3)

22 *Dahlia* 'Betty Bowen' (x 3)

23 *Schizostylis coccinea* (x 5)

24 *Tulipa* 'Queen of Night' (x 7)

shrubs

25 *Deutzia × elegantissima* (x 1)

26 *Rosa* 'Mme Isaac Pereire' (x 1)

annuals

27 *Antirrhinum majus* 'His Excellency' (x 7)

28 *Atriplex hortensis* var. *rubra* (x 5)

29 *Dianthus chinensis* 'Firecarpet' (x 5)

30 *Papaver somniferum* (x 3)

31 *Verbena* 'Showtime' (x 7)

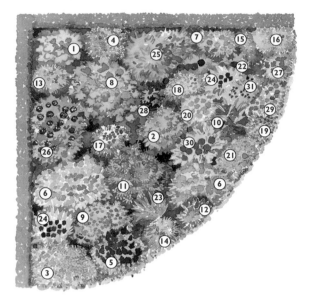

secondary colours

Introducing a second colour into what is predominantly a single-coloured border can be most effective. This may be to create a focal point or to relieve what has become a dull scene. The overall colour scheme is retained but made more interesting.

Although it may seem a simple goal, creating a border from a single colour is not easy. There are many different shades of any one colour and they do not always combine well. Yellow, for example, has two distinct forms, orange-yellows and green-yellows. Similarly, blue-reds and orange-reds are quite different in character and do not mix. There are no fixed rules for evaluating a plant's colour and it is really a question of developing an eye for blending tones.

the foliage factor

Most green leaves complement a wide range of flower colours. Variegated plants, however, should be used with caution: a strident golden variegation in the middle of this romantic pink corner bed, 3.5 x 3.5 m (12 x 12 ft), would spoil the effect completely. Similarly, silver and purple foliage can strike a jarring note unless they take up the theme of your colour scheme, so always look beyond the shade of the flower to the foliage effect to avoid disappointment. To be true to your scheme, remove any mismatched plants.

alternative scheme: a white border

The classic single-colour border is white, which produces a timeless, restful effect. Pure whites and creamy whites do not combine well, so select plants with care.

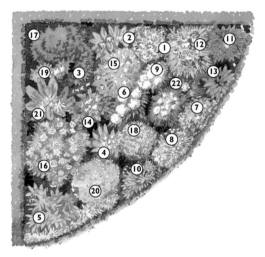

alternative planting

perennials

1 *Achillea ptarmica*
 The Pearl Group (x 3)
2 *Digitalis purpurea* 'Alba' (x 3)
3 *Anemone × hybrida*
 'Honorine Jobert' (x 3)
4 *Gypsophila paniculata*
 'Bristol Fairy' (x 1)
5 *Polygonatum × hybridum* (x 1)
6 *Phlox paniculata* 'Fujiyama' (x 1)
7 *Lamium maculatum*
 'White Nancy' (x 3)
8 *Dianthus* 'Haytor White' (x 3)
9 *Anaphalis margaritacea* (x 1)
10 *Stachys byzantina* (x 3)
11 *Smilacina racemosa* (x 1)
12 *Epilobium angustifolium*
 'Album' (x 2)
13 *Pulmonaria officinalis*
 'Sissinghurst White' (x 3)

bulbs

14 *Tulipa* 'Maureen' (x 6)
15 *Cosmos* 'Purity' (x 4)

shrubs

16 *Rosa* 'Iceberg' (x 1)
17 *Exochorda × macrantha* 'The Bride'
 (x 1)
18 *Artemisia* 'Powis Castle' (x 1)
19 *Clematis* 'Marie Boisselot' (x 1)

annuals

20 *Omphalodes linifolia* (x 5)
21 *Nicotiana sylvestris* (x 3)
22 *Antirrhinum* 'White Wonder' (x 5)

seasonal interest

The essential factor to remember for all borders is seasonal interest. A border or bed is not truly successful if its period of interest is limited to a glorious midsummer display, with nothing of significance in the spring, late summer or autumn. With single-colour beds the challenge is all the greater to find early- and late-flowering plants that take up the colour idea. This consistency is important as seasons of interest inevitably overlap.

bedding border

One of the most colourful elements of Victorian gardens was the bedding border.
Some schemes were simple, just blocks of colours, while others were complicated
designs that involved thousands of plants. By using a propagator or greenhouse
it is possible to produce all the plants required for a bedding display at minimal
cost, and the rewards are great for the minimal effort needed. Especially efffective
as front gardens, these borders will make their mark in any formal design.

PLANTING SCHEME

Cordyline australis (x 1)

Echeveria pulvinata (x 8 per m/per yd)

Echeveria secunda var. *glauca* (x 8 per m/per yd)

Sedum acre (x 150 per sq m/per sq yd)

Echeveria elegans (x 10 per m/per yd)

Alternanthera 'Aurea Nana' (x 150 per sq m/per sq yd)

Alternanthera 'Brilliantissima' (x 150 per sq m/per sq yd)

Alternanthera 'Versicolor' (x 150 per sq m/per sq yd)

Dudleya farinosa (x 12 per m/per yd)

The real skill with bedding displays is devising the design. Simple shapes can be very effective and bold while, by contrast, a complicated design will sit very well in a knot garden. A personal emblem can be incorporated into a design, or figurative elements such as butterflies and birds. Bedding plants are short-lived, so there is room for experimentation.

plants

Annuals are not the only form of bedding plant; there are countless others that work just as well, including perennials, succulents and houseplants. Think of the colours and textures you require, then look for the best candidates.

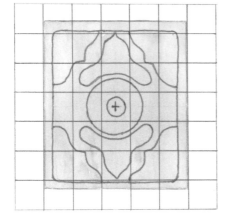

planning a bedding scheme

If the design is complicated, work it out to scale on squared paper to get the proportions right and calculate how many plants will be needed. This scheme is 6 x 3 m (20 x 10 ft), but it can be adapted to the size of your garden.

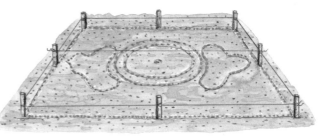

marking out the scheme

Work over the soil then mark out the design on the surface using light-coloured sand. The grid from your paper plan can be transferred using strings or long canes.

planting the bed

Assemble all your plants, making sure you have sufficient to complete the job. Starting from the middle of the bed or border and working out to the edges, plant up the design. Use a plank if necessary as a bridge from which to work. Trim and neaten the plants as you go, as you may not be able to reach the centre again.

planting scheme

1 *Cordyline australis* (x 1)

2 *Echeveria pulvinata* (x 8 per m/per yd)

3 *Echeveria secunda* var. *glauca* (x 8 per m/per yd)

4 *Sedum acre* (x 150 per sq m/per sq yd)

5 *Echeveria elegans* (x 10 per m/per yd)

6 *Alternanthera* 'Aurea Nana' (x 150 per sq m/per sq yd)

7 *Alternanthera* 'Brilliantissima' (x 150 per sq m/per sq yd)

8 *Alternanthera* 'Versicolor' (x 150 per sq m/per sq yd)

9 *Dudleya farinosa* (x 12 per m/per yd)

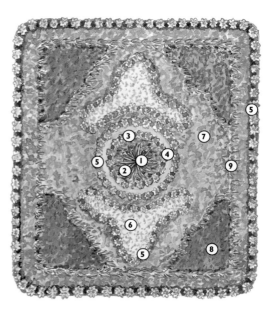

a modern touch

Bedding displays are often viewed as old-fashioned, but the wealth of plants available today and the preference for clear-cut, graphic planting make bedding ideal. A group of small beds will enliven the smallest city courtyard. Look for inspiration beyond the garden, in books on tapestry, cross-stitch or quilting (below and right).

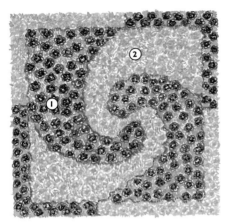

square bed

1 *Tagetes* Bonanza Series
   (x 36 per sq m/per sq yd)
2 *Tagetes* 'Vanilla'
   (x 25 per sq m/per sq yd)

diamond bed

1 *Viola cornuta* 'Victoria Cawthorne'
   (x 25 per sq m/per sq yd)
2 *Viola* 'Ardross Gem' (x 25 per sq m/per sq yd)
3 *Viola pedata* (x 25 per sq m/per sq yd)
4 *Viola* 'Huntercombe Purple' (x 25 per sq m/per sq yd)

care and maintenance

- Tender plants, as here, should not be planted out until the threat of frost is well past.
- Keep the bed weed free.
- Preserve or propagate plants for use the following year.

foliage bed

Foliage has a great advantage over flowers: it is present for most of the growing season and, in the case of evergreens, throughout the year. A foliage garden or border need never be boring. It can be a very cool, soothing place, especially if the colours, shapes and textures have been grouped in a sympathetic manner. By contrast and for a flamboyant touch, there are exotic and brightly coloured foliage plants that will create a party atmosphere and huge-leaved plants to add drama.

PLANTING SCHEME

Phytolacca americana (x 1)

Cornus controversa 'Variegata' (x 1)

Geranium macrorrhizum (x 7)

Polystichum setiferum (x 1)

Geranium palmatum (x 3)

Geranium × *magnificum* (x 3)

Iris sibirica (x 3)

Lysimachia ciliata 'Firecracker' (x 1)

Meconopsis cambrica (x 6)

Euphorbia characias subsp. *wulfenii* (x 3)

Macleaya cordata (x 3)

Romneya coulteri (x 2)

Lysichiton americanus (x 1)

Kniphofia 'Painted Lady' (x 1)

Crocosmia × *crocosmiiflora* 'Solfaterre' (x 3)

Hosta lancifolia (x 1)

Heuchera micrantha var. *diversifolia* 'Palace Purple' (x 3)

Hosta Tardiana Group 'Halcyon' (x 3)

Euphorbia dulcis 'Chameleon' (x 1)

Miscanthus sinensis (x 1)

Ferula communis (x 1)

Rodgersia podophylla (x 1)

Silybum marianum (x 3)

As all plants have leaves in one form or another, there are no limits to the mood and effect that can be created using foliage. Some plants, such as hostas and grasses, are used primarily as foliage plants. Where flowers are prominent, make sure they are an asset to the largely green scheme.

foliage forms

When choosing plants, look at the shapes of the leaves as well as their colour. A mixture of shapes is usually much more interesting than a multiplication of a single leaf form, although other qualities in the leaf – fleshy or fine, shiny or matt – should also be considered for a well-blended planting, as in this square bed, 5.4 x 5.4 m (18 x 18 ft).

planting scheme

1 *Phytolacca americana* (x 1)

2 *Cornus controversa* 'Variegata' (x 1)

3 *Geranium macrorrhizum* (x 7)

4 *Polystichum setiferum* (x 1)

5 *Geranium palmatum* (x 3)

6 *Geranium × magnificum* (x 3)

7 *Iris sibirica* (x 3)

8 *Lysimachia ciliata* 'Firecracker'
   (x 1)

9 *Meconopsis cambrica* (x 6)

10 *Euphorbia characias* subsp.
   wulfenii (x 3)

11 *Macleaya cordata* (x 3)

12 *Romneya coulteri* (x 2)

13 *Lysichiton americanus*
   (x 1)

14 *Kniphofia* 'Painted Lady' (x 1)

15 *Crocosmia × crocosmiiflora* 'Solfaterre' (x 3)

16 *Hosta lancifolia* (x 1)

17 *Heuchera micrantha* var. *diversifolia* 'Palace
   Purple' (x 3)

18 *Hosta* Tardiana Group 'Halcyon' (x 3)

19 *Euphorbia dulcis* 'Chameleon' (x 1)

20 *Miscanthus sinensis* (x 1)

21 *Ferula communis* (x 1)

22 *Rodgersia podophylla* (x 1)

23 *Silybum marianum* (x 3)

alternative scheme: a silver border

There are many colours beyond shades of green that can be used in a foliage scheme, and one of the most restful is silver. Many silver and grey plants have soft foliage and a loose, spreading habit that is excellent for an asymmetrical scheme, but they can also be very successful in a more formal planting, as in this example.

combining colours

In this design, blue and light pink flowers complement the silver foliage, lifting the overall impression made by the bed without detracting from the delicacy of the foliage shades.

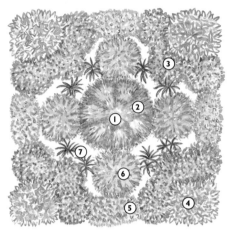

alternative planting

1 *Pyrus salicifolia* 'Pendula' (x 1)
2 *Artemisia* 'Powis Castle' (x 7)
3 *Nepeta* × *faassenii* (x 12)
4 *Stachys byzantina* (x 12)
5 *Dianthus* 'Inchmery' (x 12)
6 *Veronica spicata* subsp. *incana* (x 4)
7 *Nerine bowdenii* (x 16)

other coloured foliage

Silver is one of the few colours other than green that will sustain an entire foliage scheme. Purple foliage is very bold when it punctuates a green planting but dulling if massed. Gold and bronze are similar in their effect, while variegated plants can add confusion if used without restraint. However, all are excellent as foliage highlights.

care and maintenance

- Remove any spent flowering stems, leaving the foliage to provide the interest. The foliage of *Geranium magnificum* can be cut back as it will produce a fresh crop of leaves.
- In the autumn, remove any dead foliage and top dress with organic matter. Tie up the kniphofia foliage in a bunch above the crown to protect it.
- In the spring, remove any remaining old foliage, including that of the ferns and the kniphofia.

mixed border

The use of mixed borders has become the favourite form of ornamental gardening. Shrubs combined with perennials give a bed a sense of permanence and structure that lasts throughout the year, even during the winter months. Spring bulbs provide drifts of colour, while annuals make a most valuable contribution: they can be changed each year, thereby altering the general appearance of the border; they quickly fill gaps; and their bright colours add a touch of gaiety.

PLANTING SCHEME

Primula 'Blue Riband' (x 5)

Papaver somniferum (x 4)

Rosa gallica var. *officinalis* 'Versicolor' (x 1)

Aruncus dioicus (x 1)

Pyrus salicifolia 'Pendula' (x 1)

Delphinium 'Fenella' (x 2)

Salvia forsskaolii (x 6)

Veronica 'Shirley Blue' (x 2)

Geranium × *riversleaianum* 'Mavis Simpson' (x 1)

Leymus arenarius (x 1)

Dianthus 'Doris' (x 3)

Sisyrinchium striatum (x 4)

Baptisia australis (x 1)

Trifolium rubens (x 1)

Papaver orientale 'Mrs Perry' (x 1)

Silene dioica (x 2)

Lilium regale (x 3)

Campanula persicifolia (x 1)

Salvia sclarea (x 1)

Tanacetum vulgare (x 5)

Viola cornuta (x 3)

A wide range of perennials, shrubs and annuals can be used in this type of border. Try to use plants that are sympathetic in terms of colour and texture. Other than the short-term presence of bulbs and the changing interest given by annuals, it is very satisfying to watch a mixed bed or border mature and develop over the years. Make allowance for such growth when you plan and plant.

maintenance considerations

Mixed beds can require more attention than, say, the herbaceous or annual bed. It is possible to select plants that need little attention, but this is to discount some of the most rewarding plants that do need to be pruned, divided and protected against the elements. Decide how much time you can give to a bed before selecting the plants.

confining the leymus

Leymus is a fine plant but it spreads rapidly. Plant it in a large pot and then plunge this into the border so the rim is level with the top of the soil. Renew the soil every year.

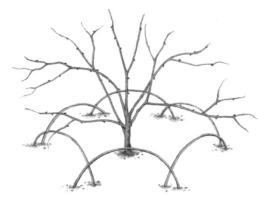

confining shrub roses

If shrub roses are left to their own devices they not only become rather loose and open in appearance but their long stems can be swept up by winds, damaging adjacent plants.

They can be controlled by tying the branches down; bending the stems also promotes flowering. Using pliable sticks such as hazel, create a circle of overlapping hoops around the rose (above) then tie the long shoots in (right).

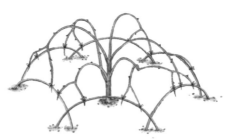

Each stem should be secured to the hoops while retaining a natural arched shape. New growth will soon hide the circle of sticks. Take the structure apart each winter, prune and retie. Remove a few of the older stems to the base to help promote new, vigorous growth.

a corner bed

This corner planting, 4.5 x 3 m (15 x 10 ft), makes a fine feature in the garden, set off by a clipped hedge.

planting scheme

1 *Primula* 'Blue Riband' (x 5)

2 *Papaver somniferum* (x 4)

3 *Rosa gallica* var. *officinalis* 'Versicolor' (x 1)

4 *Aruncus dioicus* (x 1)

5 *Pyrus salicifolia* 'Pendula' (x 1)

6 *Delphinium* 'Fenella' (x 2)

7 *Salvia forsskaolii* (x 3)

8 *Veronica* 'Shirley Blue' (x 2)

9 *Geranium* × *riversleaianum* 'Mavis Simpson' (x 1)

10 *Leymus arenarius* (x 1)

11 *Dianthus* 'Doris' (x 3)

12 *Sisyrinchium striatum* (x 4)

13 *Baptisia australis* (x 1)

14 *Salvia forsskaolii* (x 3)

15 *Trifolium rubens* (x 1)

16 *Papaver orientale* 'Mrs Perry' (x 1)

17 *Silene dioica* (x 2)

18 *Lilium regale* (x 3)

19 *Campanula persicifolia* (x 1)

20 *Salvia sclarea* (x 1)

21 *Tanacetum vulgare* (x 5)

22 *Viola cornuta* (x 3)

care and maintenance

- In spring, support the *Papaver orientale*. Other tall plants such as the tanacetum, baptisia, campanula and the delphiniums should also be supported in windy areas.
- Deadheading will promote flowering. It will also mimimize undesirable seeding.
- In the autumn, cut back all dead and dying herbaceous material, remove weeds and top dress with organic matter.
- Towards the end of the winter, prune the roses and cut out any dead wood that can be seen on the pear.

purple and yellow

Colour, both of flowers and foliage, influences the mood as well as the general appearance of a garden. Cool, pastel shades create a romantic, tranquil feel while hot colours add excitement and a sense of the exotic. Borders can be designed to contain a mixture of colours or they can use a more restrained range to striking ends. A single colour makes a strong impression but two complementary or contrasting colours can produce some of the most remarkable effects.

PLANTING SCHEME

Ligustrum lucidum 'Aureum' (x 1)

Asphodeline lutea (x 3)

Allium hollandicum (x 6)

Allium cristophii (x 3)

Helianthus 'Lemon Queen' (x 1)

Anthemis tinctoria (x 1)

Oenothera stricta (x 3)

Rosa glauca (x 1)

Cynara cardunculus (x 1)

Lupinus arboreus (x 1)

Atriplex hortensis var. rubra (x 3)

Kniphofia 'Yellow Hammer' (x 1)

Lobelia × gerardii 'Vedrariensis' (x 3)

Verbascum olympicum (x 1)

Heuchera sanguinea (x 3)

Euphorbia × martinii (x 3)

For a two-colour border, choose the plants carefully. It may be best to plan the border over several seasons, carrying a notebook to jot down suitable plants as you see them in other gardens. Shrubs, perennials, annuals and grasses can all be used to good effect; take cuttings or divide plants to ensure that the colour will come true. This 4.5 x 1.8 m (15 x 6 ft) border has year-round interest.

selecting colours

Choosing colours is a personal matter, we all have our favourites and pet hates. But before two colours are selected, certain factors should be weighed up. Does the combination work or jar? There certainly are many difficult pairings in this respect, such as red and white or orange and purple. Can the shades of the chosen plants be restricted effectively? For example, using every tone of pink could be busy enough without adding another colour. And does the combination create the desired mood?

planting scheme

1 *Ligustrum lucidum* 'Aureum' (x 1)

2 *Asphodeline lutea* (x 3)

3 *Allium hollandicum* (x 6)

4 *Allium cristophii* (x 3)

5 *Helianthus* 'Lemon Queen' (x 1)

6 *Anthemis tinctoria* (x 1)

7 *Oenothera stricta* (x 3)

8 *Rosa glauca* (x 1)

9 *Cynara cardunculus* (x 1)

10 *Lupinus arboreus* (x 1)

11 *Atriplex hortensis* var. *rubra* (x 3)

12 *Kniphofia* 'Yellow Hammer' (x 1)

13 *Lobelia × gerardii* 'Vedrariensis' (x 3)

14 *Verbascum olympicum* (x 1)

15 *Heuchera sanguinea* (x 3)

16 *Euphorbia × martinii* (x 3)

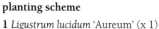

care and maintenance

- Cut the lupins back to the ground when they have finished flowering, or just remove the old flower spikes to encourage a second crop of smaller flowers.
- Cut the anthemis to the ground after flowering to encourage fresh foliage.
- Allow the self-sowing annuals and biennials limited time to seed to prevent overcrowding. Thin the resulting seedlings as they emerge.
- Cut back dead foliage in the autumn.
- Tie the kniphofia leaves in a bunch over the crown of the plant for winter protection and then cut the leaves away in the spring as the new foliage emerges.
- Top dress in the winter with well-rotted organic material.

spring planting

To provide interest in the early spring, plant daffodils and dark-coloured tulips between the existing planting. The emerging herbaceous foliage will cover the bulbs' dying leaves, but they can be cut off once they begin to turn brown.

other partners for yellow

Yellow is one of the most versatile colours in the garden. It represents a huge proportion of garden plants and works very well with other colours, in different ways.

pruning

The *Rosa glauca* in this border can be pruned heavily each spring, removing the old wood almost to the ground. This looks drastic but it will encourage new shoots with masses of richly coloured foliage.

yellow and blue

1 *Anthemis tinctoria*

2 *Helianthus* 'Lemon Queen'

3 *Kniphofia* 'Yellow Hammer'

4 *Oenothera stricta*

5 *Verbascum olympicum*

6 *Aquilegia flabellata*

7 *Eryngium × tripartitum*

8 *Aster frikartii*

9 *Delphinium* hybrids

10 *Veronica* 'Shirley Blue'

11 *Veronica longifolia*

yellow and orange

1 *Anthemis tinctoria*

2 *Helianthus* 'Lemon Queen'

3 *Kniphofia* 'Yellow Hammer'

4 *Oenothera stricta*

5 *Verbascum olympicum*

6 *Canna* 'Orange Perfection'

7 *Crocosmia × crocosmiiflora* 'Emily McKenzie'

8 *Dahlia* 'Bishop of Llandaff'

9 *Euphorbia griffithii* 'Fireglow'

10 *Geum* 'Borisii'

11 *Papaver atlanticum*

left The shapes of beds are better defined if they are outlined by a low hedge which prevents the plants flopping over the edge.

right A combination of paths and hedges weaves a tapestry in this cottage garden. The low, contained planting enhances the shapes.

shaped borders

are rewarding to create; almost any shape can be used, whether geometric or free-flowing, although sharp points are difficult to plant unless they have first been lined with a low hedge. Circular beds have elegance, a sinuous border has charm, while a parterre is the ultimate expression of order and complexity.

far left Curved, meandering lines to a border are much more interesting than a straight edge, especially when the planting is informal, as here.

above left A simple or symmetrical design featuring a central plant or ornament uses a circular bed to best advantage.

below left A clean edge between a planted border and an area of grass always helps to enhance the shape of the former.

left Large patterned areas can be most effective, especially if they can be viewed from above, as from the raised walkway over this delightful, well-planned parterre.

below left The use of shaped borders is a good approach to designing single-coloured gardens. Here, the shapes fit perfectly into the available space and set off the pattern of the brick path.

below right A circular rose bed surrounded by a gravel path: a picturesque corner of a fine garden. Small hedges extend into the circle, leading the eye towards the birdbath in the middle, an imaginative, witty device.

round bed

To many people the words 'border' and 'bed' conjure up the image of a long strip of cultivated ground but, in fact, there is no reason why a planted space should not be any shape. One of the most popular is a round bed, situated in the middle of a lawn or surrounded by a path. The symmetry of a circle is particularly effective in a formal garden; a classical approach is a group of four circular beds. By contrast, filled with annuals, the bed becomes a very gay, informal feature.

PLANTING SCHEME

Allium cristophii (x 1)
Artemisia alba 'Canescens' (x 10)
Milium effusum (x 5)
Rosa 'Ballerina' (x 5)
Scabiosa caucasica 'Clive Greaves' (x 5)
Viola, mixed pink and blue (numerous)

There are several ways of planting a round bed, depending on its role in the garden. In an informal setting, a border of mixed plants, randomly planted, can look very effective. For a formal design, order is the essential element, often with a central axis; a standard rose, planted urn or a piece of statuary.

creating the circle

There is a simple method of marking out a circular bed. Place a stake or strong stick where the centre is to be. Tie a length of string to this and at the desired diameter tie another stick. Keeping the string taut, walk round, scribing a circle in the ground.

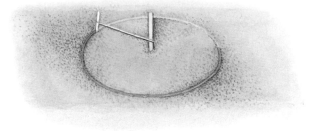

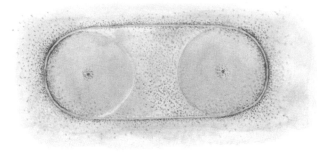

creating an oval

Another pleasing bed shape is an oval. This is easily marked out by outlining two circles (as above) and joining them with straight lines. When planning the length of such a bed, remember that the radius of the circles is an important measurement. Use a tall plant at the centre of each 'circle'.

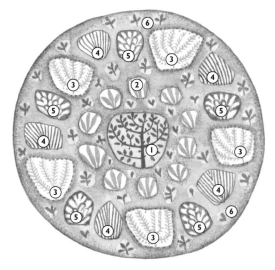

planting

As with all symmetrical schemes, the rule is to start at the centre and work outwards. Plan the bed on paper first; even a small bed can take a lot of undoing if things go wrong. This example measures 3 m (10 ft) across.

ideas for round beds

The simplest solution, well suited to a formal garden, is a bed devoted almost entirely to one variety of plant, perhaps with a single tree or bush in the centre and a low box hedge or edging around the perimeter. Alternatively, for a more contemporary look, a bold pattern can be created using bedding plants: a jagged gash of colour across the bed or a series of concentric circles.

planting scheme

1 *Allium cristophii* (x 1)
2 *Artemisia alba* 'Canescens' (x 10)
3 *Milium effusum* (x 5)
4 *Rosa* 'Ballerina' (x 5)
5 *Scabiosa caucasica* 'Clive Greaves' (x 5)
6 *Viola*, mixed pink and blue (numerous)

alternative planting

1 *Stachys byzantina* (x 4)

2 *Salvia patens* (x 60)

3 *Salvia fulgens* (x 60)

4 *Heliotropium arborescens*
  'P. K. Lowther' (x 60)

alternative scheme: a wheel

One of the most effective ways to plant up a round bed is to create a spoked wheel, with a central pivot, radiating bands and planted 'spaces' and an edging, each containing a single variety of plant. Use colour wisely, with a restricted palette of complementary tones.

care and maintenance

- With closely planted beds such as these, it is important to keep plant growth neat, otherwise the bed can look crowded and unkempt.
- Tread carefully to cause minimal disturbance when pruning a standard rose or topiary centrepiece.

parterre

Although parterres may seem only to belong to stately homes, many a small town
garden contains one, scaled down and designed to enhance the size and shape available.
In essence, a parterre is a formal arrangement of beds to form a geometric or more
fluid pattern. Typically, the edges are delineated by low hedges or brickwork, with
the enclosed spaces filled with plants in contrasting colours. The results are
pleasing to the eye and at their best provide year-round interest.

PLANTING SCHEME

Buxus sempervirens 'Suffruticosa' (9 per m/per yd)
Sedum 'Herbstfreude' (4 per sq m/per sq yd)
Begonia × carrierei 'Red Ascot' (36 per sq m/per sq yd)
Nicotiana langsdorffii (9 per sq m/per sq yd)
Verbena 'Blue Lagoon' (9 per sq m/per sq yd)

There is no right or wrong way to create a parterre. The designer's imagination can run free, making the pattern as simple or as complicated as desired. Although curves soften a design, an entirely straight-edged parterre can be very successful. Much of the overall impact of a parterre lies in the viewing and it will always make more of a mark if viewed from above, from a terrace or window.

a formal parterre

Much of the challenge in producing a beautiful traditional parterre lies in the plant selection. Starting with the framework, the best growing border is dwarf box but other good candidates include lavender – with the bonus of its fragrance – santolina and teucrium. Traditionally, each bed should be made up of plants of a single colour or sometimes two colours. Annuals allow for and demand a yearly change, while small shrubs form a permanent planting. High on the list should come antirrhinum, begonias, diascias, impatiens, lobelia, salvias, tagetes and violas. Parterres do not have to be large. This fine one is 6 x 4.5 m (20 x 15 ft).

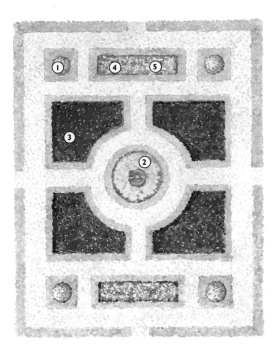

planting scheme

1 *Buxus sempervirens* 'Suffruticosa' (9 per m/per yd)
2 *Sedum* 'Herbstfreude' (4 per sq m/per sq yd)
3 *Begonia × carrierei* 'Red Ascot' (36 per sq m/ per sq yd)
4 *Nicotiana langsdorffii* (9 per sq m/per sq yd)
5 *Verbena* 'Blue Lagoon' (9 per sq m/per sq yd)

care and maintenance

- Keep the box hedging well trimmed.
- Keep gravel paths well raked.
- Do not make the contained beds too large, otherwise planting and trimming will be very difficult.

brick parterre

In marked, and some might say refreshing, contrast are brick-based parterres. These are ideal for smaller city gardens and are the answer for anyone seeking the order and impact of a parterre without waiting years to see hedging at its best. Much, but by no means all, of the interest lies in the pattern in the brickwork. The same principles apply as for traditional planted parterres when filling beds: use blocks of colour or single plants. If space is limited, a clever and witty approach is to fill the compartments with vegetables and herbs. In this way, a modern courtyard can become a traditional herb garden.

alternative planting

1 onions	10 red lettuce
2 Swiss chard	11 pak-choi
3 lettuce	12 courgettes
4 chives	13 radishes
5 leeks	14 runner beans
6 parsley	15 carrots
7 Brussels sprouts	
8 beetroot	
9 cabbages	

shapes

Parterres have taken all manner of shapes over the centuries. Favourite devices are trompe l'oeil effects, with 'overlapping' beds, and dynamic curlicues. All were conceived in the name of elegance, formality, style and wit.

corner planting

All gardens have odd corners, and since most gardeners complain that they never have enough space, it makes sense to use all these pockets. Another advantage of filling these corners is that it helps to unify the garden, to create an overall picture. A common solution is to use bland ground-cover plants to fill such areas but it is far better to create something interesting like this simple cool-looking border. Make every inch count.

PLANTING SCHEME

Alchemilla alpina (x 9)

Euphorbia stricta (x 4)

Mimulus guttatus (x 3)

Deschampsia flexuosa (x 2)

Geranium pratense 'Mrs Kendall Clark' (x 1)

Alchemilla conjuncta (x 1)

One way to deal with small corners is to fill them with containers of plants, but, while this is useful in paved areas, there is far less work – particularly with watering – if the plants are put into a properly prepared bed. Such small and often awkwardly shaped beds need to be treated with particular imagination and then they will play their part in the whole garden picture.

a gravel finish

Gravel is a very useful garden material. It is a mulch, complements many plants and presents an orderly finish. It can make a highlight of a corner planting, as with this 3.5 x 3.5 m (12 x 12 ft) plot. Alternatively, use paving slabs and plant between them, creating a tapestry of cover. Erigeron, acaena, thyme and mint are useful; the last two are also aromatic.

care and maintenance

- If planting close to a wall, avoid using tall plants that may bend forwards, drawn to the light and pushed by winds.
- Make sure the gravel is well distributed around the plants and that any small rocks are securely bedded in the ground.

planting scheme

1 *Alchemilla alpina* (x 9)

2 *Euphorbia stricta* (x 4)

3 *Mimulus guttatus* (x 3)

4 *Deschampsia flexuosa* (x 2)

5 *Geranium pratense* 'Mrs Kendall Clark' (x 1)

6 *Alchemilla conjuncta* (x 1)

alternative scheme: a small rock garden

A well-constructed, well-planted rock garden is an excellent solution for many corners. The rule is to bury at least half of each rock in the soil. This will make it secure and provide a cool, moist rootrun. Arrange rocks in tiers, all leaning back slightly.

safety considerations

Never lift more than you can comfortably handle and protect your fingers from crushing stones. Get help if necessary. Move large rocks using a strong pole as a lever or roll rather than lift them. Make sure all rocks are secure.

alternative planting scheme

1 *Daphne tangutica* (x 1)
2 *Juniperus communis* 'Compressa' (x 1)
3 *Picea mariana* 'Nana' (x 1)
4 *Helianthemum* 'Annabel' (x 1)
5 *Phlox douglasii* 'Crackerjack' (x 1)
6 *Aubrieta* 'Joy' (x 1)
7 *Euphorbia myrsinites* (x 1)
8 *Lewisia tweedyi* (x 2)
9 *Erinus alpinus* (x 1)
10 *Dianthus* 'Little Jock' (x 1)
11 *Rhodohypoxis baurii* (x 10)
12 *Armeria juniperifolia* (x 1)
13 *Pulsatilla vulgaris* (x 1)
14 *Androsace carnea* subsp. *laggeri* (x 1)
15 *Achillea clavennae* (x 1)
16 *Gentiana septemfida* (x 1)
17 *Convolvulus althaeoides* (x 1)
18 *Sisyrinchium idahoense* subsp. *bellum* (x 1)
19 *Hypericum olympicum* 'Citrinum' (x 1)
20 *Campanula carpatica* (x 1)
21 *Aster alpinus* (x 1)
22 *Geranium cinereum* subsp. *subcaulescens* (x 1)
23 *Dianthus* 'Annabel' (x 1)
24 *Polygala chamaebuxus* var. *grandiflora* (x 1)
25 *Erodium corsicum* (x 3)

designing a rock garden

Rock gardens are intended to replicate rocky outcrops so aim for strata of rocks, leaning at the same slight angle into the ground.

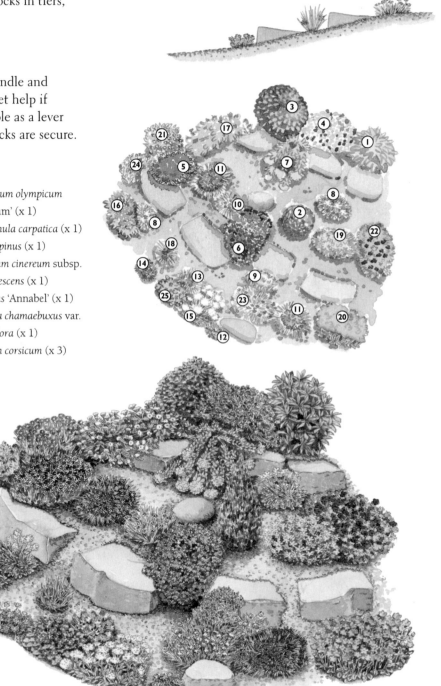

care and maintenance

- Weed rock gardens regularly, as once weeds have taken hold they can be difficult to remove.
- The top dressing of gravel will gradually mix into the soil: replace as necessary.
- Cover any plants that may suffer from winter cold with a sheet of glass or a frame covered with polythene, but allow air to circulate at the sides.
- Water alpines during dry spells.
- Trim back straggling plants.

special borders

give the garden a distinctive and often unusual character. From enlivening dry and shaded sites to lifting a pond display, these borders often include plants and materials quite different from those seen in traditional beds.

left Waterside planting can include an exuberant mixture of foliage and flowering plants, presenting luxuriant displays. Here, white lilies shine out against clumps of spreading foliage.

right Candelabra primulas are extremely good plants for wet and boggy areas. Both their colour and shape create interest and are seen at their best against still, bright water.

below Some wetland plants, such as this *Iris ensata*, can be grown in an ordinary border if a pond is not available, providing they have plenty of moisture-retaining compost.

above Shady and woodland borders have a peaceful, protected quality. Hellebores, hepaticas and cyclamen are all ideal for such conditions.

above left Grasses are wonderful plants for the varied form and colour of their foliage and for their sheer versatility and hardiness. They are an asset in dry beds.

above right Succulent plants, such as this spiny agave, will thrive in dry Mediterranean-style growing conditions. Gravel creates a perfect background for drought-tolerant plants, particularly architectural specimens that deserve space to be admired.

centre A subtle variation in colours is always worth attempting. The result can be very cool and satisfying, as in this dry, green and yellow border.

right In areas where rainfall has declined it has become essential to change to plants that will grow happily in dry conditions. The diversity of suitable plants, often very dramatic in appearance, confirms that a dry climate does not mean dull gardens.

waterside planting

Water features add a special dimension to a garden. A soothing sound as a stream trickles or pool ripples, lively or leisurely movement and subtle reflections or darts of light; all are irresistible to any gardener. Such features allow and call for a lush planting of fresh colours, both in the flowers and the foliage. The whole environment around a water feature creates a tranquillity that is rarely reproduced elsewhere in the garden.

MATERIALS AND EQUIPMENT

spade

PVC or butyl membrane pond liner to size

soft builder's sand

bricks

well-rotted compost

topsoil

slabs of inverted turf

lattice pots for plants to be planted in the pond

plants for the ledge (see right)

PLANTING SCHEME

Iris pseudacorus 'Variegata' (x 1)

Iris sibirica (x 6)

Ranunculus lingua (x 5)

Phalaris arundinacea (x 3)

Typha latifolia (x 3)

Hosta sieboldiana var. *elegans* (x 1)

Hosta tokudama f. *flavocircinalis* (x 1)

Mimulus luteus (x 3)

Hydrocharis morsus-ranae (x 3)

Nymphaea 'René Gérard' (x 1)

Primula pulverulenta (x 2)

Salix babylonica (x 1)

Although many of the plants grown beside a pond can also be grown in a border, most particularly enjoy moist soil. Avoid plants that prefer dry conditions – these include most silver-foliaged plants. Those that grow in shallow water at the edge and in the pond should be true aquatic plants.

creating a waterside border

Dig out the pond to the shape required, including a ledge around the edge; this will carry the waterside border. Slope the ledge outwards to encourage the absorption of water from the pool. Cover the whole surface with a layer of soft builder's sand to about 5 cm (2 in) in depth, to prevent sharp objects penetrating the liner.

lining the pond and border

Stretch the liner across the pond so that it extends well beyond the ledge. Place bricks around the edge to keep it stretched and fill the pond. The liner will sink, taking up the profile of the hole, dragging the bricks inwards. Fill the liner to the edge of the ledge. Ease the material into the contours of the ledge and tuck the liner firmly into the bank so that it is concealed.

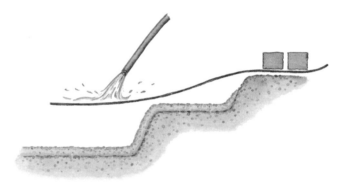

making the border

Build a wall of inverted turf, forming a bank. Fill the space behind this with a mixture of topsoil and well-rotted compost. Allow the soil to settle, then add more water to the pond so that it soaks into the border. If the soil in the border sinks, top it up.

planting the bed

When planting an edging bed on top of a liner, be very careful not to damage the material when digging. Carefully dig holes and insert the plants. Plant those that require most water, or that will grow with their roots in water, at the edge of the pond. To add variety to the scheme, suitable plants can be placed in the pond itself, in special lattice pots. This full scheme is 3 x 6 m (10 x 20 ft).

planting scheme

1 *Iris pseudacorus* 'Variegata' (x 1)
2 *Iris sibirica* (x 6)
3 *Ranunculus lingua* (x 5)
4 *Phalaris arundinacea* (x 3)
5 *Typha latifolia* (x 3)
6 *Hosta sieboldiana* var. *elegans* (x 1)
7 *Hosta tokudama* f. *flavocircinalis* (x 1)
8 *Mimulus luteus* (x 3)
9 *Hydrocharis morsus-ranae* (x 3)
10 *Nymphaea* 'René Gérard' (x 1)
11 *Primula pulverulenta* (x 2)
12 *Salix babylonica* (x 1)

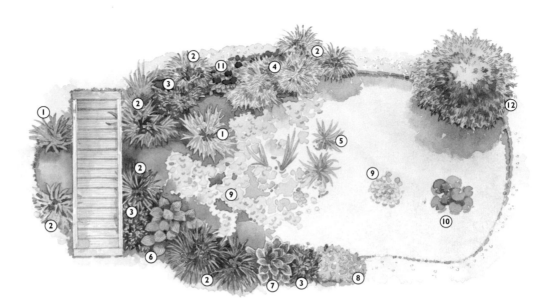

care and maintenance

- Weeds love lush, moist conditions and must be hunted out and removed constantly, otherwise they can overrun a planting scheme, making it look neglected.
- Cut back dead foliage in the autumn and top dress the edging bed with organic matter such as garden compost or leafmould.
- Many waterside plants are rampant and need to be removed every two or three years. Replant just a few pieces.
- When maintaining the border, be careful not to puncture the liner.
- Check the condition of the liner regularly, looking for any exposed or damaged areas.

dry border

Gardeners throughout the world are facing a shortage of water so it is a good idea
to make the most of plants that are used to growing in dry regions. Just as attractive
as plants from more temperate areas, their more contained growth habits and foliage
forms can give a border a more architectural appearance. For a neat finish, the ground
can be mulched with small stones. These will help preserve moisture and keep down
weeds, making the border easy to maintain.

TOOLS AND MATERIALS

spade
tamper
roller
large stones for underlayer
small stones for path
path edging (optional)

PLANTING SCHEME

Penstemon heterophyllus (x 5)
Asphodeline lutea (x 3)
Persicaria affinis (x 5)
Juniperus scopulorum
'Skyrocket' (x 1)
Eryngium giganteum (x 8)
Stipa gigantea (x 1)
Sedum 'Vera Jameson' (x 3)
Phormium tenax (x 1)
Artemisia 'Powis Castle' (x 1)
Verbena bonariensis (x 7)

Sedum telephium subsp.
maximum 'Atropurpureum'
(x 3)
Allium hollandicum 'Purple
Sensation' (x 7)
Stachys byzantina (x 3)
Pennisetum villosum (x 1)
Agapanthus 'Ben Hope' (x 1)
Euphorbia dulcis 'Chameleon'
(x 3)

The beauty of drought-tolerant plants is that they need very little attention once established. For the best results, dig over the empty bed in the autumn, adding well-rotted organic material to improve the soil and some sharp sand or fine grit. Together, these additions will help to lighten the soil. Any rain should then rapidly soak through.

a suitable path

Paths made of gravel or small stones not only make a good surface on which to walk but also provide a good setting for dry-loving plants.

making a gravel path

To make a stony path, first remove all weeds and, depending on the size of the path, tamp (right) or roll the surface down for a compact, level finish.

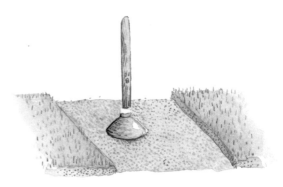

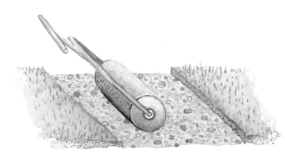

Cover the prepared base with a layer of stones, 2.5 cm (1 in) deep. This should be rolled well into the base (left).

Another method is to dig out the path to a depth of 2.5–5 cm (1–2 in), level it, roll it, and then lay black plastic garden sheeting (right). Bury the edges into the soil on either side of the path.

Finally, for both methods, cover with a loose layer of stones at least 2.5 cm (1 in) deep. Edge the path with wood, stone or bricks (left), or leave the sides vague to merge with the bed.

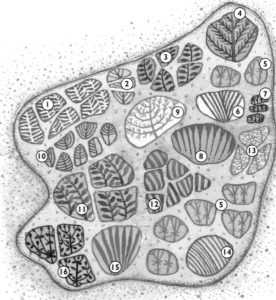

planting scheme

1 *Penstemon heterophyllus* (x 5)

2 *Asphodeline lutea* (x 3)

3 *Persicaria affinis* (x 5)

4 *Juniperus scopulorum* 'Skyrocket' (x 1)

5 *Eryngium giganteum* (x 8)

6 *Stipa gigantea* (x 1)

7 *Sedum* 'Vera Jameson' (x 3)

8 *Phormium tenax* (x 1)

9 *Artemisia* 'Powis Castle' (x 1)

10 *Verbena bonariensis* (x 7)

11 *Sedum telephium* subsp. *maximum* 'Atropurpureum' (x 3)

12 *Allium hollandicum* 'Purple Sensation' (x 7)

13 *Stachys byzantina* (x 3)

14 *Pennisetum villosum* (x 1)

15 *Agapanthus* 'Ben Hope' (x 1)

16 *Euphorbia dulcis* 'Chameleon' (x 3)

alternative scheme: succulents

Succulents are ideal for dry conditions, giving a garden a healthy display of lush plants, typified by fleshy leaves. As with the main planting, this irregular bed, which is approximately 5.4 x 5.4 m (18 x 18 ft), is surrounded by an informal gravel path.

alternative planting

1 *Cotyledon orbiculata* (x 3)

2 *Dorotheanthus bellidiformis* (x 10)

3 *Jovibarba hirta* (x 10)

4 *Rhodiola rosea* (x 4)

5 *Sedum acre* (x 20)

6 *Sedum aizoon* 'Euphorbioides' (x 8)

7 *Sedum lydium* (x 5)

8 *Sedum spathulifolium* 'Aureum' (x 6)

9 *Sedum spectabile* 'Meteor' (x 3)

10 *Sedum spurium* 'Schorbuser Blut' (x 5)

11 *Sedum telephium* subsp. *maximum* 'Atropurpureum' (x 3)

12 *Sedum* 'Bertram Anderson' (x 6)

13 *Sedum* 'Herbstfreude' (x 5)

14 *Sedum* 'Morchen' (x 3)

15 *Sedum* 'Ruby Glow' (x 3)

16 *Sedum* 'Sunset Cloud' (x 6)

17 *Sedum* 'Vera Jameson' (x 6)

18 *Sempervivum* 'Commander Hay' (x 10)

19 *Sempervivum* 'Glowing Embers' (x 4)

20 *Sempervivum* 'Lady Kelly' (x 5)

21 *Sempervivum tectorum* (x 6)

22 *Yucca flaccida* (x 1)

23 *Yucca gloriosa* 'Variegata' (x 1)

24 *Yucca filamentosa* 'Ivory' (x 1)

care and maintenance

- Ensure that the bed remains well drained.
- Many dry-loving plants produce decorative seedheads, which can be kept for autumn interest.

woodland border

Woodland borders conjure up a romantic image of beautiful flowers in wide, misty glades surrounded by luxuriant trees, an image well beyond most gardens. However, the idea can be carried out on a much smaller scale with surprising success. Such a border only needs one or two trees to provide the shade and atmosphere, while the smaller plants create the effect. Indeed, there is no reason why the whole could not be miniaturized and created under a few large shrubs.

TOOLS AND MATERIALS

spade
tamper
roller
logs
sticks
bark chippings

PLANTING SCHEME

Rosa 'Ramona' (x 1)
Corylus avellana (x 1)
Hosta Tardiana Group
'Halcyon' (x 1)
Geranium × *magnificum* (x 3)
Dicentra 'Bountiful' (x 5)
Iris sibirica (x 1)
Geranium pratense (x 1)
Alchemilla mollis (x 2)
Bergenia 'Silberlicht' (x 3)
Brunnera macrophylla (x 1)

Campanula latifolia (x 1)
Digitalis purpurea (x 5)
Epimedium × *rubrum* (x 1)
Euphorbia amygdaloides var.
robbiae (x 3)
Helleborus foetidus (x 3)
Myosotis sylvatica (x 3)
Persicaria affinis (x 3)
Pulmonaria officinalis (x 3)
Stylophorum diphyllum (x 2)
Tellima grandiflora (x 3)

Woodland borders extend from under trees where the conditions range from dense to mottled shade. The number of plants that will tolerate full shade is limited, although this can be overcome in the spring when the sparser tree canopies allow more light through. For the rest of the year, use the woodland margins to provide colour and interest.

woodland conditions

Trees and shrubs are notoriously hungry and thirsty plants, so the soil should be well provided with plenty of well-rotted organic compost. In keeping with a natural setting, this is best provided by leafmould made by composting any available foliage after it has fallen in the autumn. After clearing any weeds, dig the proposed border, adding as much leafmould as possible. This will help the soil to retain moisture, but the border will never be as wet as a bed in open ground, so choose plants that will tolerate dryness. Plant in the autumn on lighter soils but wait until the spring if the soil is at all heavy. This border is 4.5 x 4.5 m (15 x 15 ft).

creating a bark path

Paths around a woodland border or through shady areas are best kept informal. A natural material for such paths is bark chippings, itself a woodland product. This gives a soft finish and particularly suits meandering paths. To make the path, first consolidate the soil below the intended path (see page 56).

The sides of a bark path can be left vague to blend into the borders, or the path can be edged with logs to prevent the bark spreading too far. If logs are used, hold them in place by inserting sticks at intervals on either side.

Pour 5–7 cm (2–3 in) of bark chippings along the path. If it is much deeper than this the path will be too soft. Rake at regular intervals and top up with fresh bark as the material breaks down into humus.

woodland bulbs

In spring, before the leaves appear on the trees, woodland areas are often full of bulbs, making the most of the sunlight before leafy canopies darken the ground. Many spring bulbs are suitable for woodland use. The best way to achieve a random planting is to scatter the bulbs onto the ground and plant them where they fall. The depth of planting varies but as a rule of thumb always plant three times the depth of the bulb. Snowdrops should be planted while they are 'in the green', that is, while they are still in growth, just after flowering and while their leaves are green.

planting scheme

1 *Rosa* 'Ramona' (x 1)
2 *Corylus avellana* (x 1)
3 *Hosta* Tardiana Group 'Halcyon' (x 1)
4 *Geranium* × *magnificum* (x 3)
5 *Dicentra* 'Bountiful' (x 5)
6 *Iris sibirica* (x 1)
7 *Geranium pratense* (x 1)
8 *Alchemilla mollis* (x 2)
9 *Bergenia* 'Silberlicht' (x 3)
10 *Brunnera macrophylla* (x 1)
11 *Campanula latifolia* (x 1)
12 *Digitalis purpurea* (x 5)
13 *Epimedium* × *rubrum* (x 1)
14 *Euphorbia amygdaloides* var. *robbiae* (x 3)
15 *Helleborus foetidus* (x 3)
16 *Myosotis sylvatica* (x 3)
17 *Persicaria affinis* (x 3)
18 *Pulmonaria officinalis* (x 3)
19 *Stylophorum diphyllum* (x 2)
20 *Tellima grandiflora* (x 3)

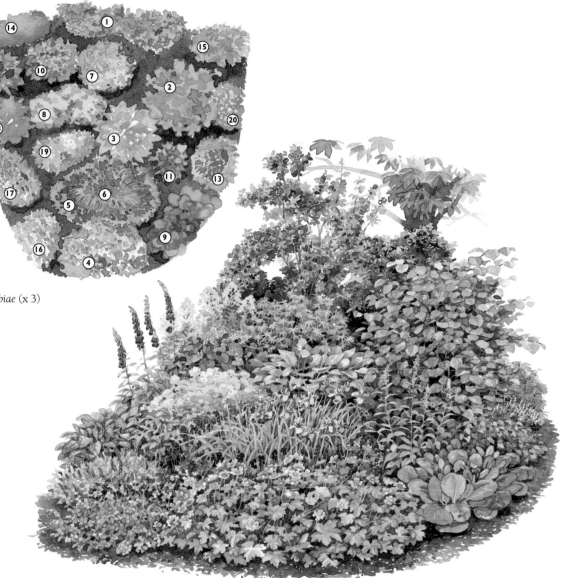

spring underplanting

To enhance spring interest, there are many plants that can be added under and around the main plants. Many of these spring-flowering plants will run to seed, forming a most desirable carpet of colour.

spring planting

1 *Anemone nemorosa* (x 4)
2 *Convallaria majalis* (x 4)
3 *Cyclamen coum* (x 8)
4 *Eranthis hyemalis* (x 4)
5 *Galanthus nivalis* (x 20)
6 *Hyacinthoides non-scripta* (x 12)
7 *Narcissus pseudonarcissus* (x 6)

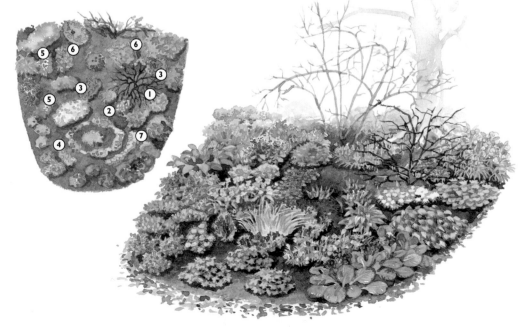

mediterranean border

In areas where hot, dry summers are the norm, there is little
point in trying to create a lush herbaceous border that
prefers cooler conditions. A Mediterranean border is the ideal solution,
with plants that are colourful both in their flowers and foliage.
Hardy plants, they will succeed in cooler regions where a rather
exotic look is desired.

TOOLS AND MATERIALS

spade

tamper

roller

large stones for underlayer

small stones for path

PLANTING SCHEME

Veronica 'Shirley Blue' (x 6)

Cistus × skanbergii (x 1)

Chamaecyparis lawsoniana
'Pembury Blue' (x 1)

Althaea officinalis 'Romney
Marsh' (x 3)

Onopordum acanthium (x 3)

Euphorbia characias (x 1)

Cistus × fernandesiae 'Anne
Palmer' (x 2)

Nectaroscordum siculum (x 25)

Allium unifolium (x 25)

Lavandula officinalis (x 1)

Sedum 'Herbstfreude' (x 3)

Stachys byzantina (x 10)

Ballota pseudodictamnus (x 3)

Salvia × superba 'Superba'
(x 2)

Lychnis coronaria (x 1)

Salvia jurisicii (x 1)

Acaena saccaticupula 'Blue
Haze' (x 12)

Salvia officinalis
'Purpurascens' (x 2)

Linaria purpurea 'Springside
White' (x 1)

Papaver somniferum (x 5)

The Mediterranean border has diversity and warmth of colour, yet presents quite a different quality from the plants most familiar to temperate climates. They are resilient against dry heat and a surprising degree of cold and make few demands; excellent for low-maintenance gardening.

creating a mediterranean border

Prepare the bed first then lay the path. Dig over the plot in the autumn, removing any perennial weeds and adding well-rotted organic material. Mediterranean plants like ground that does not remain too wet, so if the soil is heavy clay add sharp sand or fine gravel to help with drainage. In the spring, fork over the soil and break it down with a rake, removing any weeds that have appeared over winter. The most suitable pathing is gravel, which can be left to blend with the edges of the border as here (see page 56 for construction). This curved site is around 4.5 x 3 m (15 x 10 ft).

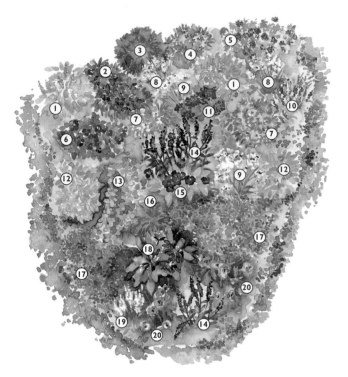

care and maintenance

- Trim back plants after flowering.
- Some of the seedheads, such as the alliums and the onopordum, make good dried flowers and can be kept in the border or picked for indoor use.

planting scheme

1 *Veronica* 'Shirley Blue' (x 6)

2 *Cistus* × *skanbergii* (x 1)

3 *Chamaecyparis lawsoniana* 'Pembury Blue' (x 1)

4 *Althaea officinalis* 'Romney Marsh' (x 3)

5 *Onopordum acanthium* (x 3)

6 *Euphorbia characias* (x 1)

7 *Cistus* × *fernandesiae* 'Anne Palmer' (x 2)

8 *Nectaroscordum siculum* (x 25)

9 *Allium unifolium* (x 25)

10 *Lavandula officinalis* (x 1)

11 *Sedum* 'Herbstfreude' (x 3)

12 *Stachys byzantina* (x 10)

13 *Ballota pseudodictamnus* (x 3)

14 *Salvia* × *superba* 'Superba' (x 2)

15 *Lychnis coronaria* (x 1)

16 *Salvia jurisicii* (x 1)

17 *Acaena saccaticupula* 'Blue Haze' (x 12)

18 *Salvia officinalis* 'Purpurascens' (x 2)

19 *Linaria purpurea* 'Springside White' (x 1)

20 *Papaver somniferum* (x 5)

a dry stream-bed

In dry areas the garden can be enhanced by taking elements of the Mediterranean landscape and incorporating them into the border. For example, the impression of a dry stream-bed can be created through the centre of the border.

dry-stream planting

1 *Miscanthus sinensis* (x 1)

2 *Cordyline australis* (x 1)

3 *Agapanthus* 'Bressingham Blue' (x 1)

4 *Ophiopogon planiscapus* 'Nigrescens' (x 6)

5 *Euphorbia characias* subsp. *wulfenii* (x 1)

6 *Eryngium giganteum* (x 3)

7 *Callistemon citrinus* (x 1)

dry-stream planting

The most appropriate scheme is a sparse planting of grasses and drought-tolerant plants with a jumble of pebbles, smooth rocks, water-worn wood and old tree stumps lining a shallow gully.

collecting seed

Many of the plants in this bed produce seed. When ripe, the seedpods turn brown or black and the seeds fall away freely when lightly moved. Tip the seed or the whole seedhead into a labelled paper bag. Place in a warm airy place where the contents of the bag can dry, but not in a hot place and especially not in sunlight. When dry, sieve the seed to remove detritus then empty them into a labelled envelope. This can be kept in the refrigerator until required.

shady border

Many gardens have a shady corner, perhaps in the shadow of an overhanging tree
or caused by adjacent walls or fences. In some cases the shade may be dense,
in others there may be light from above but the area is never reached by direct
sunlight. This situation is one of the most difficult to deal with in gardening terms,
as most flowering plants need sunshine to give of their best. However, there are
ways of using these areas to advantage.

PLANTING SCHEME

Hosta Tardiana Group 'Halcyon' (x 1)

Hosta fortunei var. *aureomarginata* (x 1)

Euphorbia characias subsp. *wulfenii* (x 1)

Nectaroscordum siculum (x 10)

Nepeta racemosa (x 3)

Tanacetum parthenium (x 6)

Lilium martagon (x 1)

Smyrnium perfoliatum (x 5)

Tellima grandiflora (x 3)

Geranium nodosum (x 1)

Lamium galeobdolon (x 3)

Hemerocallis 'Pink Damask' (x 1)

Drypoteris filix-mas (x 1)

Carex pendula (x 1)

Foeniculum vulgare (x 1)

Hyacinthoides non-scripta (x 10)

Shade usually works hand in hand with other problems. Walls, trees and similar objects not only cast a sun shadow but a rain shadow; this means that the border is deprived of moisture as well as light. An area between two buildings or structures might also be a draughty location, as whirling currents of air can be created along alleyways even on apparently windless days.

overcoming problems

The right choice of plants will minimize the problem of lack of sunlight and the moisture content of the soil can be improved by the addition of well-rotted organic material (see page 60) and a mulch. Strong winds can be moderated by using resilient shrubs as windbreaks, or a built screen. Where part of a border does get the sun, add sun-loving plants; here, in this 1.8 x 3.5 m (6 x 12 ft) bed, nepeta is included.

an ivy corner

A simple but imaginative idea is to fill the shady area with ivy, not in the style of a neglected garden but as a living sculpture. Add surfaces and contours to the space with mounds of earth, tree stumps or even objects such as old metal chairs, then plant the ivy at 45 cm (18 in) intervals and allow it to ramble freely. The vigorous nature of the plant will come into its own.

other plants for shade

Anemone nemorosa	*Lilium martagon*
Arum italicum	*Meconopsis betonicifolia*
Aruncus dioicus	*Omphalodes cappadocica*
Astilbe	*Omphalodes verna*
Cardiocrinum giganteum	*Oxalis acetosella*
Convallaria majalis	*Pachysandra terminalis*
Cornus canadensis	*Polygonatum × hybridum*
Corydalis flexuosa	*Primula*
Cyclamen coum	*Smilacina racemosa*
Eranthis hyemalis	*Trillium*
Euphorbia amygdaloides	*Vancouveria chrysantha*
Galanthus nivalis	*Vinca minor*
Helleborus orientalis	*Viola odorata*
Houttuynia cordata	
Iris foetidissima	(see also Woodland Border,
Kirengeshoma palmata	pages 58–61)
Lathyrus vernus	

planting scheme

1 *Hosta* Tardiana Group 'Halcyon' (x 1)
2 *Hosta fortunei* var. *aureomarginata* (x 1)
3 *Euphorbia characias* subsp. *wulfenii* (x 1)
4 *Nectaroscordum siculum* (x 10)
5 *Nepeta racemosa* (x 3)
6 *Tanacetum parthenium* (x 6)
7 *Lilium martagon* (x 1)
8 *Smyrnium perfoliatum* (x 5)
9 *Tellima grandiflora* (x 3)
10 *Geranium nodosum* (x 1)
11 *Lamium galeobdolon* (x 3)
12 *Hemerocallis* 'Pink Damask' (x 1)
13 *Drypoteris filix-mas* (x 1)
14 *Carex pendula* (x 1)
15 *Foeniculum vulgare* (x 1)
16 *Hyacinthoides non-scripta* (x 10)

planting a north wall

Not all gardens can be south- or west-facing, and one of the worst situations in gardening terms is a north wall. This suffers from prolonged or constant shade and, as a result, a marked chilliness when compared to other parts of the same garden. Such an unpropitious microclimate can still see plantlife that will cheer a dull corner.

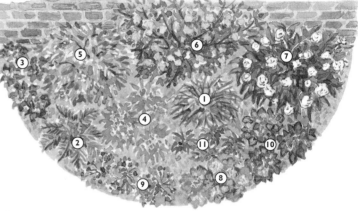

full-shade planting

1 *Carex pendula* (x 1)

2 *Dryopteris filix-mas* (x 1)

3 *Cyclamen hederifolium* (x 5)

4 *Euphorbia amygdaloides* var. *robbiae* (x 3)

5 *Garrya elliptica* (x 1)

6 *Rosa* 'New Dawn' (x 1)

7 *Camellia japonica* (x 1)

8 *Alchemilla mollis* (x 1)

9 *Geranium macrorrhizum* (x 3)

10 *Epimedium × versicolor* 'Sulphureum' (x 3)

11 *Hyacinthoides hispanica* (x 4)

rose bed

Roses are still among the most popular of garden plants. Not only do they provide
the garden with masses of beautiful flowers but they also frequently fill it with the
most delightful fragrance. Roses are very versatile. They can be grown as ground
cover, as low, medium or tall bushes, around pillars or obelisks or allowed
to scale trellis and even trees. They can be combined with other plants
or used to create a unique feature, the rose garden.

PLANTING SCHEME

Rosa 'Pink Grootendorst' (x 1)
Salvia greggii (x 5)
Geranium palmatum (x 5)

ALTERNATIVE MODERN SHRUB ROSES

'Charles Austin' (apricot and yellow)   'Glamis Castle' (white)   'Othello' (crimson)

'Constance Spry' (pink)   'Golden Celebration' (yellow)   'The Countryman' (pink)

'Cottage Rose' (pink)   'Graham Thomas' (yellow)   'Warwick Castle' (pink)

'Dark Lady' (deep red)   'Heritage' (pink)   'Wife of Bath' (pink)

'English Garden' (yellow)   'L. D. Braithwaite' (crimson)   'Winchester Cathedral' (white)

'Gertrude Jekyll' (pink)   'Mary Rose' (pink)

A rose is such an impressive, complete plant that a bed using a single variety can work very well, and if the plant becomes large, then even a single specimen can be used. Here, the large rugosa rose, 'Pink Grootendorst', creates a centrepiece around which a small selection of perennials is placed. These are planted tight against the rose so they merge to form a bold mound.

choosing roses

There are literally thousands of roses to choose from and probably the best way to choose is to visit a specialist nursery while they are in flower. Various factors influence a gardener's selection: flower colour and fragrance, whether the plant is repeat-flowering and the ultimate size of the variety are four key elements. For a relatively confined space, as with this 2.4 m (8 ft) bed, size is a significant point.

planting roses

Prepare the soil and plant. Bare-rooted roses should be planted between autumn and early spring. This is also the best time for planting container-grown plants, although they can be planted any time if kept watered.

plant associations

Some gardeners like to see bare earth under their roses. However, for an abundant look, there are many plants that work well with roses, including alliums, anthemis, diascia, fragaria, geraniums, persicaria, pulmonaria, stachys and violas. The best place for these companion plants is around the margins, where they can both be seen and benefit from the sun.

planting scheme
1 *Rosa* 'Pink Grootendorst' (x 1)
2 *Salvia greggii* (x 5)
3 *Geranium palmatum* (x 5)

alternative modern shrub roses

'Charles Austin'

'Cottage Rose'

'Winchester Cathedral'

'Golden Celebration'

'Heritage'

'Constance Spry'

alternative scheme: an obelisk

Rose beds can consist of just shrub roses or they can include low climbers trained up an obelisk or pillar. More vigorous varieties will swamp a pergola or a long trellis (see page 79). The use of attractive garden structures such as these can enhance the impact of the plants.

alternative planting

1 *Rosa* 'Alister Stella Gray' (x 1)
2 *Rosa* 'Graham Thomas' (x 4)
3 *Tropaeolum majus* 'Alaska' (x 8)

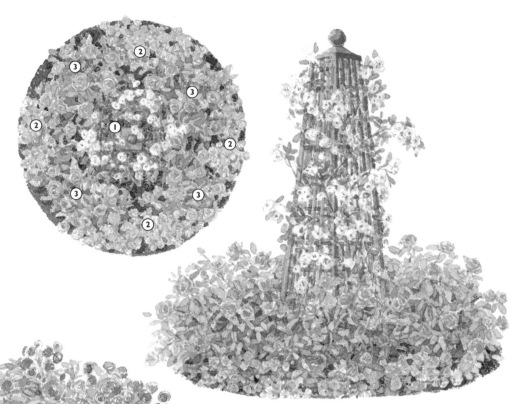

care and maintenance

- To get the best results from roses, prune regularly.
- Be on your guard against diseases, such as black spot, rose rust and powdery mildew, and pests, such as aphids.

walkthrough borders

are highly sensuous as they allow the viewer to get right among the plants. This creates a greater intimacy with their sight, feel and smell. Where arches or pergolas are involved, the viewer is totally surrounded by plants and their fragrance. All gardeners should allow time to walk through their borders.

above This very romantic prospect comprises a formal paved promenade lined with borders contained behind box hedges. The whole is framed by a series of arches covered in roses and clematis.

below A walled garden filled with a profusion of old-fashioned cottage-garden plants. The narrow path just allows the visitor to wander through the

flowers, brushing and smelling as they go. The discreet path adds to the sense that this is a secret garden.

right Wide paths created from irregular-sized paving slabs run between square and rectangular beds. The shapes are formal but the planting, by contrast, is exuberant, asymmetrical and filled with life.

above Beautiful formality is enhanced by the simplicity of this design. Identical beds spread onto a grass pathway with a central stream gully. The stone edging directs the eye clearly along the straight line while the purple and green add a lively quality.

below The silky heads of this grass, *Hordeum jubatum*, just ask to be caressed as you walk along the central path. They contrast nicely with the cleome beyond.

above A curve in a path adds a note of mystery to any garden scene. Here, a stretch of grass curves away, suggesting a great garden beyond.

left Paths within a path: here, bold stepping stones lead in opposite directions while the main grass track forges ahead. Each possibility demands exploration.

edible border

Most of the produce for the kitchen comes from the vegetable and herb gardens, but there is plenty that can be grown in the more ornamental parts of the garden. Some flowers can be eaten or used as a garnish to food, while many vegetables are so decorative they more than earn their place in the borders. Creating a border with culinary value as well as decorative worth can be very enjoyable and provides great economy of space in a small garden.

PLANTING SCHEME

Atriplex hortensis 'Rubra' (red mountain spinach: edible young leaves) (x 60)
Calendula officinalis (pot marigold: edible flowers) (x 30)
Cynara cardunculus (cardoon: edible blanched stems) (x 6)
Helianthus annuus (sunflower: edible seed) (x 20)
Hemerocallis (daylily: edible opening buds) (x 8)

Although the major concern of this border is decorative, many of the elements are made up from edible plants. While tradition dictates that vegetable and flower gardens are kept separate, there is no reason why this should be so.

The unexpected presence of decorative vegetables can give a freshness to a planting. The soil for such a border needs no different preparation than any other border and the planting and maintenance are just the same.

planting scheme

1 *Atriplex hortensis* 'Rubra' (red mountain spinach: edible young leaves) (x 60)

2 *Calendula officinalis* (pot marigold: edible flowers) (x 30)

3 *Cynara cardunculus* (cardoon: edible blanched stems) (x 6)

4 *Helianthus annuus* (sunflower: edible seed) (x 20)

5 *Hemerocallis* (daylily: edible opening buds) (x 8)

edible ornamentals

All the edible plants in this border will enhance a salad, while the opening buds of the daylily can be chopped up and stir-fried. These beds are 6 x 1.8 m (20 x 6 ft) but, if space is limited, all the more reason to include edibles.

warning

Not all garden plants are edible and only those known to be safe should be eaten or used as food decoration.

edible flowering plants and vegetables

The list of plants that are edible in whole or part is very long. Here are some of the most rewarding, both in terms of their decorative qualities and for culinary purposes. The less familiar edible parts of some popular flowers are pointed out.

vegetables
carrots (foliage)
Swiss chard (foliage)
tomatoes (fruit)
peas (flowers and fruit)
sweetcorn (foliage)
lettuce (bronze foliage)

flowering plants
Mentha (mint: leaves)
Viola odorata (sweet violets: flowers)
Tropaeolum majus (nasturtium: flowers)
Thymus (thyme: leaves)
Borago officinalis (borage: flowers)
Rosa (roses: petals)
Rosmarinus officinalis (rosemary: flowers, leaves)

pergola planting

A pergola, be it a substantial wooden structure or a more refined metal frame, should complement the pathway borders; here, use edible plants.

using the pergola

The pergola straddling the path allows the addition of several types of vegetables or fruit. The overall effect is that of an avenue of produce through which a shady walk can be taken. For a temporary display, runner beans, climbing French beans or marrows and courgettes can be grown. For a more permanent display, grapes (right), apples or pears can be trained over the arches, or a combination of apples and pears (above). Keep the climbers well trained and pruned to get the best from them. This should also allow more light to reach the plants in the borders than if the climbers are neglected.

care and maintenance

• Where only parts of plants are being harvested, take from a different plant each time so that there is time for regrowth and you do not create an unbalanced appearance in the bed.

cottage-garden path

The wealth of plants in a traditional cottage garden creates a wild, romantic air. A riot of colours and shapes speaks of the informality of a typical country border, and it can be created in any garden if the whole scheme is sympathetic to this freely planted approach. For those who like an unpredictable display, this is the perfect path-side look.

PLANTING SCHEME

year-round interest

Juniperus communis 'Depressa Aurea' (x 1)

spring flowering

Erysimum (x 7)

Forsythia (x 1)

Narcissus (x 19)

Primula vulgaris (x 8)

Tulipa (x 16)

Viola × *wittrockiana* (x 5)

summer flowering

Achillea ptarmica The Pearl Group (x 3)

Alcea rosea (x 8)

Alchemilla mollis (x 6)

Dianthus 'Mrs Sinkins' (x 6)

Digitalis purpurea (x 5)

Echinops ritro (x 3)

Erigeron 'Serenity' (x 3)

Erodium manescaui (x 1)

Geranium himalayense (x 3)

Hemerocallis fulva (x 3)

Lavandula angustifolia (x 1)

Lychnis coronaria (x 3)

Lysimachia punctata (x 3)

Lysimachia nummularia 'Aurea' (x 3)

Oenothera biennis (x 6)

Papaver somniferum (x 6)

Phlox 'Cherry Pink' (x 6)

Rosa rugosa (x 1)

Stachys byzantina (x 3)

Trollius europaeus (x 1)

Viola cornuta (x 3)

The charm of the original Victorian cottage gardens lay in the fact that they were simply a wonderful collection of plants. With little knowledge of the niceties of garden design, cottage gardeners freely filled gaps in a border and allowed annuals to seed unhindered, creating a busy picture of fruit, vegetables and native ornamentals.

planning a cottage garden

When laying out a cottage garden, a sense of freedom should be maintained. For an authentic touch, only traditional plants (pre-c.1900) should be used, although the spirit of a cottage garden will allow any colourful plants to be included providing they do not need too much cosseting. Fruit and vegetables should also be included if possible.

practicalities

Aside from the useful presence of edible plants, cottage gardens exhibited other practical characteristics. Tight planting prevented weeds from growing, while the use of a wide range of robust plants helped to prevent any one pest or disease causing wholesale damage.

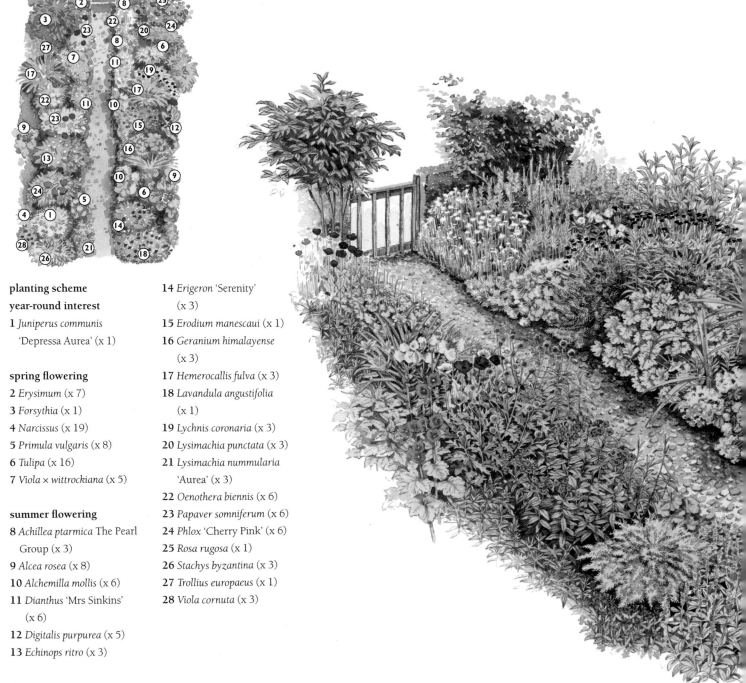

planting scheme

year-round interest

1 *Juniperus communis* 'Depressa Aurea' (x 1)

spring flowering

2 *Erysimum* (x 7)

3 *Forsythia* (x 1)

4 *Narcissus* (x 19)

5 *Primula vulgaris* (x 8)

6 *Tulipa* (x 16)

7 *Viola × wittrockiana* (x 5)

summer flowering

8 *Achillea ptarmica* The Pearl Group (x 3)

9 *Alcea rosea* (x 8)

10 *Alchemilla mollis* (x 6)

11 *Dianthus* 'Mrs Sinkins' (x 6)

12 *Digitalis purpurea* (x 5)

13 *Echinops ritro* (x 3)

14 *Erigeron* 'Serenity' (x 3)

15 *Erodium manescaui* (x 1)

16 *Geranium himalayense* (x 3)

17 *Hemerocallis fulva* (x 3)

18 *Lavandula angustifolia* (x 1)

19 *Lychnis coronaria* (x 3)

20 *Lysimachia punctata* (x 3)

21 *Lysimachia nummularia* 'Aurea' (x 3)

22 *Oenothera biennis* (x 6)

23 *Papaver somniferum* (x 6)

24 *Phlox* 'Cherry Pink' (x 6)

25 *Rosa rugosa* (x 1)

26 *Stachys byzantina* (x 3)

27 *Trollius europaeus* (x 1)

28 *Viola cornuta* (x 3)

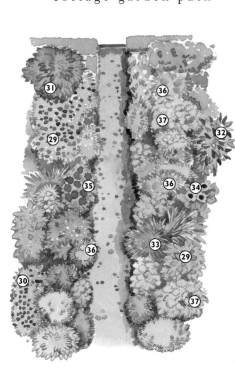

maturing time

These pathway borders are 9 x 4 m (30 x 13 ft) and will begin to mature in two years, although shrubs will take many years to reach their ultimate size.

late summer and autumn interest

The cottage garden should provide interest throughout the year. Although many plants in this border flower for a short period, their foliage is long-lived. Some plants blur the boundaries by flowering repeatedly over a long period or have a second flowering in the autumn.

late-season planting

29 *Anemone × hybrida* (x 4)
30 *Aster novae-angliae* 'Andenken an Alma Pötschke' (x 5)
31 *Aster novi-belgii* (x 3)
32 *Buddleja davidii* (x 1)
33 *Crocosmia masoniorum* (x 6)
34 *Helianthus annuus* (x 5)
35 *Sedum spectabile* (x 3)
36 *Solidago* 'Cloth of Gold' (x 4)
37 *Tanacetum vulgare* (x 3)

care and maintenance

* Make sure that any tall or flopping plants are well supported. It will be difficult to reach them once the border is in full growth.
* While abundant growth can be very attractive, take care paths are not made dangerous by trailing, slippery stems.

alternative pathways

As with all garden styles, the appearance of the path can alter the impression made by the cottage garden.

bricks

A simple brick pattern and attractive weathering suit the country style.

grass

Introduce patterns by setting the lawn mower at different heights.

stepping stones

Stones bedded in beaten earth lead the eye along the path.

scented path

Borders that line paths are always welcome as they bring the viewer close to the plants. This is doubly rewarding with fragrant borders as the sense of smell as well as that of sight is stimulated; in many cases, the action of rubbing against the plants as you pass produces the fragrance. Lavender and rosemary have very distinctive, strong aromas that pervade the air for a long distance, far beyond the pathway.

SCENTED PLANTS

fragrant foliage	fragrant flowers	
Aloysia triphylla	*Berberis*	*Lupinus*
Artemisia	*Choisya ternata*	*Matthiola*
Lavandula	*Convallaria majalis*	*Nicotiana*
Mentha	*Daphne*	*Osmanthus*
Monarda didyma	*Dianthus*	*Philadelphus*
Myrtus communis	*Erysimum*	*Reseda odorata*
Origanum	*Hesperis matronalis*	*Rhododendron* (azaleas)
Rosmarinus	*Hyacinthus*	*Rosa*
Salvia officinalis	*Iris unguicularis*	*Sarcococca*
	Lathyrus odoratus	*Syringa*
	Lilium	*Viburnum*
		Viola odorata

Fragrant plants should be used more frequently in the garden as they add a special dimension to it. While there are some plants that are positively fetid, there are many that produce the most wonderful perfumes, such as lavender. These are perfect for creating a relaxing atmosphere, the raison d'être of many a garden today. This delightful path is 7.5 x 2.5 m (25 x 9 ft).

design

It is important that a path is sufficiently wide for its purpose. Most garden paths should be wide enough for two people to walk side by side; an allowance of at least 1.5 m (5 ft) should be made. Paths that are purely for access can be narrower but should still take a wheelbarrow comfortably.

preparing and planting the beds

Using a string line as a guide, plant the lavenders in a straight row, each being close enough to the next to merge with it when in full growth, that is 60 cm (2 ft) all round. To make a consistent picture, use the same coloured variety for all the plants. Seed-grown plants may be cheaper but the colours can vary. Plant the shrubs to the same depth as they were in their pots, firm down and water. If possible, mulch the plants to retain moisture and to keep down weeds.

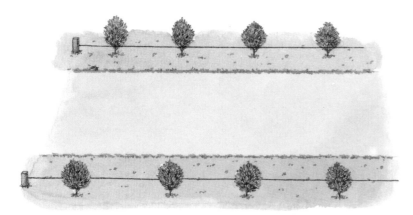

care and maintenance

• Lavender should be sheared over in late summer. Remove all flower stems and cut away about 2.5 cm (1 in) of the previous season's growth. Shape the border into a slightly undulating, low hedge (right).

alternative pathway

Cottage-style gardens have paths over which everything seems to spill. Paths for this kind of border should be wide enough to accommodate both the spreading plants and the passage of people. Typical fragrant plants for this type of display are the border pinks, especially the old-fashioned varieties.

alternative planting

1 *Lupinus* 'Kayleigh Ann Savage' (x 1)

2 chives (x 3)

3 *Dianthus* 'Haytor White' (x 1)

4 thyme (x 1)

5 sage (x 1)

6 *Dianthus* 'Gran's Favourite' (x 2)

7 *Artemisia caucasica* (x 1)

8 *Alchemilla mollis* (x 2)

9 *Geranium sanguineum* 'Album' (x 1)

10 mint (x 1)

11 *Dianthus* 'Laced Monarch' (x 1)

12 *Tanacetum parthenium* 'Aureum' (x 1)

courtyard path

In small paved gardens there seems to be little choice but to grow plants in pots. However, for a larger display, a generous raised bed is ideal as it will hold sufficient soil to sustain a number of plants, both permanent perennials and seasonal annuals. As well as presenting the prospect of more versatile planting schemes, raised beds also create different levels, which add interest to the space. If they border a path, the extra height can be used to display angular and trailing foliage.

TOOLS AND MATERIALS

spade	grass turves or a sheet of
trowel	horticultural polythene
hardcore	bricks, stone or concrete blocks
concrete	timbers or railway sleepers
crocks or stones	(no foundations needed)

PLANTING SCHEME

Corylus maxima 'Purpurea' (x 1)
Phormium tenax 'Purpureum' (x 4)
Heuchera micrantha var. *diversifolia* 'Palace Purple' (x 8)

Raised beds are not difficult to create and once filled with soil they can be treated like any other border, with the full range of plants that that implies. They allow great scope for the garden designer, but it is essential to plan and build these structures carefully if they are to fit and work well in a garden.

materials

A variety of materials can be considered for building a raised bed: brick, as here, stone, concrete blocks and wood. Wood is possibly the easiest to use, especially if old railway sleepers can be found; these are heavy baulks of timber that make sturdy walls. They are longer lasting than other forms of wood as they have been impregnated with tar, but therein lies their drawback: in hot conditions they ooze tar.

foundations

Brick, stone and concrete blocks are used in the same way. If the bed is not to be built on a solid base, foundations should be dug, to a depth of about 25 cm (10 in). A 10 cm (4 in) layer of hardcore should be rammed into this, topped by a 15 cm (6 in) layer of concrete. The wall is built on top of this.

drainage

It is most important that drainage holes are left in the lower levels of the brickwork to allow excess water to drain away. A few gaps in the vertical pointing are usually sufficient.

finishing details

For brick walls, a line of tiles can be added towards the top (right). This detail is not essential, but partly decorative and partly to direct water away from the wall, so that the surface is not stained by repeated drenchings.

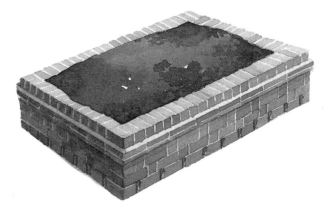

before planting

To aid drainage, add broken crocks or stones to a depth of 7 cm (3 in) or more, then a layer of upturned turves (above) or horticultural polythene with drainage holes. Fill with good quality loam with plenty of well-rotted organic matter and some grit to help drainage (left). Firm down as you go and overfill, as the soil will sink with time.

planning

A courtyard, with its strong architectural identity, lends itself to symmetrical, well-blended displays and plants with bold foliage forms. So plan raised beds accordingly, using plants that will stand up to close scrutiny as people walk along the path: full foliage and fragrance are assets. This large raised bed is 3.6 x 2.5 m (12 x 8 ft).

planting scheme

1 *Corylus maxima* 'Purpurea' (x 1)
2 *Phormium tenax* 'Purpureum' (x 4)
3 *Heuchera micrantha* var. *diversifolia* 'Palace Purple' (x 8)

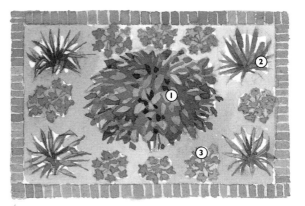

care and maintenance

- Keep the soil in raised beds topped up and check that the structure is draining efficiently.

railway sleepers

Sleepers are laid directly onto a flat base. When using them, stagger the vertical joins, as with brickwork, to give a firmer finish. Leave small gaps for drainage. Remember to lift the timbers with care as they are heavy.

traditional stone

Slabs of light brown and grey stones give quite a different finish to a wall of bricks. They are particularly well suited to cottages and country houses and, if the house is of stone, ideally the same local material should be used.

rose-trellis walk

For a garden to be successful it needs to benefit from different heights and contours.
A meandering trellis covered in plants makes a beautiful feature that draws the eye
above the ground and can lead it to a picturesque detail, perhaps a fountain, bench
or sympathetically planted bed. When the trellis travels the length of a pathway
it can also be enjoyed on a leisurely stroll; add the romance and sweet fragrance
of roses and you will have made a favourite part of any garden.

PLANTING SCHEME

Rosa 'American Pillar' (x 3)

Rosa 'Félicité Perpétue' (x 2)

Geranium 'Johnson's Blue' (x 32)

Rosa 'Constance Spry' (x 2)

Rosa 'L. D. Braithwaite' (x 3)

ALTERNATIVE ROSES

climbers and ramblers

'Albéric Barbier' (yellow and white)

'Alister Stella Gray' (yellow and white)

'Blush Noisette' (pink)

'Cécile Brünner' (pale pink)

'Leverkusen' (lemon yellow)

'Mme Alfred Carrière' (white)

'Maigold' (yellow)

'New Dawn' (pink)

'Paul's Himalayan Musk' (pale pink)

'Paul's Scarlet Climber' (scarlet)

'Sanders' White Rambler' (white)

'Seagull' (white)

'Veilchenblau' (purple)

'Zéphirine Drouhin' (pink)

shrubs

'Charles Austin' (apricot and yellow)

'English Garden' (yellow)

'Gertrude Jekyll' (pink)

'Glamis Castle' (white)

'Graham Thomas' (yellow)

'Heritage' (pink)

'Mary Rose' (pink)

'Othello' (crimson)

'The Countryman' (pink)

'Warwick Castle' (pink)

'Winchester Cathedral' (white)

Trellis is a traditional garden structure that continues to have great appeal. Its versatility and ease of use make it an asset in gardens of any size. The simple, open structure of rustic trellising allows light through while giving ample support to climbing plants. Always remember the underplanting to give the trellis an abundant, balanced appearance.

a rose walkway

A trellis running the length of a path is an excellent device. It gives structure to a design and height across the garden, not just at the edges. For a rose walkway, think of repeat-flowering climbing or rambling varieties; these will give a longer season. There is no reason why the roses should be restricted to one type; each section can be different or two roses can be mixed in one section. If the walk is narrow then 'Zéphirine Drouhin', which is thornless, makes a good choice. This trellis bed is 7.5 x 1.2 m (25 x 4 ft).

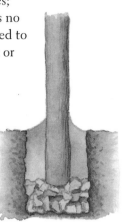

erecting a trellis

Make sure the structure is strong as it will have to carry the weight of the roses and also withstand the impact of any wind. The posts must be secure in the ground, in a hole 60 cm (2 ft) deep, bedded on hardcore and fixed with concrete (above). For a solid finish, it is important that the top beam and diagonals fit tightly into generous notches at each joint (left), strengthened with nails or screws.

shrub rose border

To complement the trellis, a border of shrub roses can be planted on the other side of the path. The colours should be sympathetic to those on the trellis but the bushes should be lower so that other parts of the garden can be seen from the walk. The whole will create a prospect of dense roses.

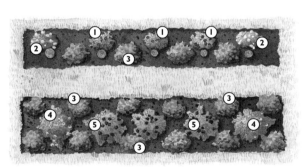

underplanting

The soil can be left bare under both the trellis and the shrub border, although more interest is created if they are underplanted. This will also help keep weeds down. Keep the planting simple; do not choose too many different plants, one variety may well be sufficient. These plants should be a finishing touch; the roses are the chief glory.

planting scheme
1 *Rosa* 'American Pillar' (x 3)
2 *Rosa* 'Félicité Perpétue' (x 2)
3 *Geranium* 'Johnson's Blue' (x 32)
4 *Rosa* 'Constance Spry' (x 2)
5 *Rosa* 'L. D. Braithwaite' (x 3)

alternative trellising

A very attractive version can be made by linking the tops of the uprights with a thick piece of rope. Additional lengths of rope will give the roses extra support. Tie in the roses as they climb and look out for stray stems that might swing across the walk. These should be well secured to prevent accidents.

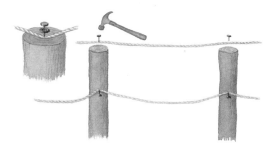

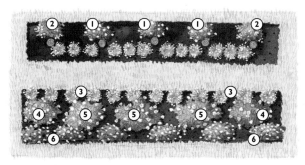

alternative scheme: a white walkway

The perennial favourite is a white scheme. For freshness and purity nothing can match it. If space is limited, white also has an advantage over stronger colours, which can dominate a garden scene. There are scores of beautiful white roses to choose from.

alternative planting

1 *Rosa* 'Mme Alfred Carrière' (x 3)

2 *Rosa* 'Seagull' (x 2)

3 *Dianthus* 'Mrs Sinkins' (numerous)

4 *Rosa* 'Winchester Cathedral' (x 2)

5 *Rosa* 'Glamis Castle' (x 3)

6 *Geranium sanguineum* 'Album' (numerous)

basic techniques

SOIL PREPARATION

The most important aspect of creating a border is thorough preparation. Without it, even the best designs are likely to fail after a year or two, smothered by weeds or starved of nutrients and moisture.

Remove all perennial weeds before planting. Even a small piece of root will re-emerge as a weed, by which time it might be difficult to remove without digging out the whole border again. In lighter soils it may be possible to dig the soil and remove weeds at the same time, while on heavier soils it may be necessary to use a weedkiller; if so, always follow the directions on the packet. Dig the soil in the autumn and plant in the spring. This will allow any small piece of weed left in the soil to reveal itself so that it can be removed. In areas with warmer winters it is also possible to dig in spring and plant in autumn.

DOUBLE-DIGGING

All borders should be dug over but they will be better, especially on heavy soils, if they are double-dug so that the lower spit of earth is also broken up. Do not dig if the soil is too wet. As the border is dug, as much well-rotted organic matter should be incorporated into the soil as possible. This not only improves the structure of the soil but provides nutrients for the plants. Its fibrous nature also helps to preserve moisture deep in the soil where the plants' roots need it. Consequently, when double-digging it is important to add generous quantities of organic material to the lower spit. Once the soil has been dug over, leave it for several months. This will allow the rain and frost to break it down and kill any pests. Residual weeds will also reappear. Avoid walking on the area while it is weathering.

double-digging
1 Dig a trench, 30–45 cm (12–18 in) wide and 30 cm (12 in) deep. Save the removed earth.

2 Work the trench for a further 30 cm (12 in) and add organic matter. Dig out the next trench and use the earth to fill the first.

3 As before, work through the layer below, breaking up the ground with a fork and adding organic material.

4 When you have reached the end of the border, fill the final trench with the earth removed from the first trench.

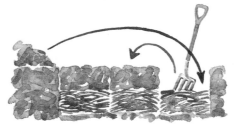

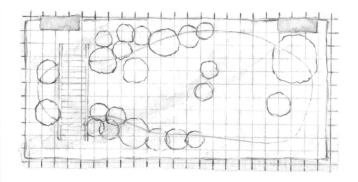

SOIL CONDITIONERS

Chipped or composted bark Best used as a mulch
Commercially prepared conditioners Good
conditioners but expensive
Farmyard manure Good all-round conditioner as long
as it does not contain weed seed
Garden compost Good all-round conditioner as long
as it does not contain weed seed
Leaf mulch Excellent conditioner and mulch
Peat Little nutrient value and breaks down too quickly
to be of great value
Seaweed Excellent conditioner that includes plenty
of minerals
Spent hops Good conditioner but limited nutrients
Spent mushroom compost Good conditioner and
mulch; includes lime

GARDEN COMPOST

One of the best ways of
providing organic material
for the garden is to make
your own compost. Almost
all plant material can
be used if it is not too
woody or contains weed
seed (woody material
can be used once it has
been shredded). Avoid diseased material or virulent
weeds, but uncooked vegetable waste from the kitchen
is recommended.

Place all the material in a container that has air holes
in the sides. Avoid creating too thick a layer of any one
material, such as grass cuttings. Keep the bin moist but
covered so that the compost retains heat and to avoid
it becoming too wet and chilled in heavy rain. Turn the
heap occasionally.

If possible, have two bins: one for collecting material and
one in use. Three is even better, the extra bin rotting down.

PLANNING

When planning a border, or even a whole garden, there are
several basic points to consider before you begin to draw
up a plan. The first is to assess what you want to achieve.
You may, for example, want a low-maintenance border, or
a bright, fun border, or a romantic display in pastel tones;
plenty of flowers for cutting might be a priority, or you
might prefer a largely foliage effect.

Next, look at where you want to put the border and
consider its physical attributes. Does it get plenty of sun
or is it in perpetual shade? Is the soil acid or alkaline?
Is it wet or dry or just about right? Is it heavy or sandy?
All these factors will have a bearing on how much work
you will have to put in and on what plants you can and
cannot grow. For example, if you live on a chalky soil you
will not be able to grow rhododendrons.

After this, decide what plants you want to use to create
the desired effect. This is best done over at least one season
so that you can go round gardens, notebook in hand,
compiling a list of desirable plants. Looking through books
also provides plenty of ideas. Having compiled your list
of plants, it is important to find out whether you can get
them locally or if you will have a long search. Adjust your
list accordingly.

You are now ready to plot the planting. Using squared
paper, draw out the border to scale and then mark out the
plants, drawing them at their eventual spread (above).
You do not need to be a good draughtsman. Adjacent
colours should be sympathetic and the border should have
an even spread of interest throughout the year. It is a good
idea to draw the bed at different seasons so you can judge
the success of the plan, and from the front to compare the
plants' relative heights. If problems appear through these
sketches, it is so much easier to correct them on paper
than after planting.

PLANTING

Before planting, rake or lightly fork over the soil, taking
care to remove any weeds that have appeared. If only a
small amount of organic material was added when the
soil was being prepared, a light dressing of a general
fertilizer can be raked into the surface. Always follow
the directions on the packet.

Do not plant in extremes of weather, that is, too hot,
wet or cold. The best time for planting shrubs and trees is
from late autumn to early spring, and for perennials either
autumn or spring. Tender annuals should be planted out
only after the threat of frost has passed. Plant hardy
annuals in autumn or spring.

Position the plants, still in their pots, on the border to get some visual idea of how the display will look (below). Make any adjustments you think necessary. Dig a hole wider than each plant's rootball and insert the plant so that it is at the same depth as it was in its pot or, if it is bare-rooted, in its previous bed. If the roots have become pot-bound or tangled, gently tease them out and spread them in the hole. Fill the hole and firm the soil around the roots.

When planting trees and shrubs, dig a much larger hole than the plant's rootball and dig plenty of well-rotted organic material into the bottom of the hole (below). Also mix some into the soil that will go back into the hole once the plant is in place. If staking the tree or shrub, position the stake before planting so that the roots will not be damaged by the stake driving through them.

USING A MULCH

Once all the plants are in the bed, water them thoroughly, rake over the surface to level it off and then apply a mulch. Mulches cover the surface of the soil, helping to keep the moisture in, preventing weed seed germinating and preventing the surface of the soil panning (hardening), which would restrict air and moisture. It can also create an attractive background against which to display the plants.

There are two types of mulches, organic and inorganic. Organic ones consist of chipped bark, leafmould, spent mushroom compost or even grass cuttings and straw.

The last two are unattractive but are valuable in areas that cannot be seen, such as the backs of borders. Inorganic ones include plastic sheeting (which is ugly and should be covered with soil, gravel or other stones), gravel or pebbles. Gravel is good for alpine beds and dry borders.

MAINTENANCE

The best borders are those that are well maintained. Issues such as staking, pruning and watering must be considered.

staking

Always stake plants that could blow over or become top-heavy in rain. There are many ways to stake perennials. Tall flower spikes can be supported by individual canes, while clumps can be held by pea sticks, netting supported between posts or by proprietary linking stakes. Stake plants when they are half-grown; do not wait until they blow over.

Trees and shrubs should be staked with a single or double stake. For most trees it is sufficient to use a single tie low down, 30 cm (12 in) from the ground. For standards and spindly trees use a taller stake and two ties.

pea stick supports
These are versatile, flexible supports that can be drawn together and tied to form a supporting case around vulnerable plants. They can be removed easily.

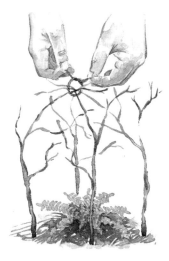

netting support
A net support is a permanent device. The plant grows up and through the mesh which, in time, will be hidden by foliage.

string and stakes

Stakes with a network of strings are useful as a temporary support for larger, spreading shrubs until they are established.

staking trees

A single tie should be placed low down to support a tree. This will give sufficient extra stability until the tree is established.

staking standard bushes

Standards need a taller stake than most trees and two ties (the first tie is shown here, positioned high up the stem).

dead-heading

As a general rule, always cut off any dead or dying flowers, unless you want to collect the seed or save the seedheads for decoration. Many perennials, such as nepeta, a number of geraniums, alchemilla and oriental poppies, should be cut to the ground after flowering; this will encourage a fresh crop of leaves to grow and the plant will then be useful for foliage effect.

watering

Water plants in dry conditions, making certain that they get a thorough soaking, the equivalent of at least 2.5 cm (1 in) across the surface. Do not water in full sun. Feeding

should not be necessary if the border is top dressed regularly. Every autumn, fork in the organic mulch and replace it with a layer of farmyard manure or garden compost. In the spring, dig this into the border and reapply the usual mulch.

weeding

Remove any weeds on sight. Regular checks will keep weeds under control; if left they can become difficult and time-consuming to eradicate. With conscientious application it should be possible to weed a border by hand. Chemical herbicides should be avoided on a planted area.

autumn care

In the autumn, most perennials should be cut back. This task can be left until the spring so that the old stems give some protection to the crown from frosts, although tidying during the dormant season means that there is less to do during the spring rush.

pruning

Ornamental trees and evergreen shrubs generally do not need pruning, except to remove any dead or dying branches, although stems can be removed for aesthetic reasons. By contrast, most deciduous shrubs benefit from regular attention. The aim is to keep the bush healthy and vigorous so that it produces good foliage and flowers. To do this, up to a third of the old wood should be cut out

removing old, dead and weak wood

A shrub like the one at right should be thoroughly pruned. Dead and weak wood should go and some of the old stems.

pruning cuts

Correct pruning cuts are very important to the health of plants. Cuts should be sloping, just above a viable bud (above, far left).

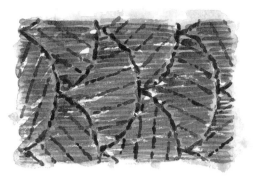

direct sowing: annuals
If clumps of plants are required, mark out the ground with fine sand before sowing.

direct sowing: perennials
1 Dig the soil well then rake it over to produce a fine tilth for sowing.

2 Make a shallow drill with the edge of a hoe, using a guide line if necessary. This can be made from pegs and a length of string.

3 Pour some water into the drill. This will help to consolidate the hollow and ensure the seeds receive adequate moisture.

4 Sow the seed, sprinkling a fine line into the shallow trench. Do not overfill as overcrowding can starve seedlings of nourishment.

5 Draw the soil back into the drill with the back of the rake and lightly water in.

each year, encouraging new growth. As a general rule, the best time to prune is immediately after the bush has finished flowering. Diseased, dead or weak growth should also be removed. Pruning cuts should be sloping, just above a viable bud.

SOWING SEED

There are two ways of sowing seeds, directly in the soil and into trays or pots (see illustrations above).

direct sowing
If sowing annuals into a border, break the dug soil into a fine tilth with a rake. If several clumps of plants are required, mark each area with sand so you can see where to sow. Scatter the seed over the required area and gently rake in. Water with a fine-rosed watering can. If sowing perennials in a seed bed, draw out a shallow drill with the edge of a hoe, using a guide line if necessary. Damp the soil and sprinkle seed along it. Draw the soil back into the drill and water.

pot sowing
If only a few plants are required or if it is necessary to sow the seed in gentle heat, they should be sown in a tray or pot. Using a good seed compost, fill the pot and tap it on the bench to settle the contents; level and lightly press it down. Sow the seed thinly and cover with a layer of fine grit or compost. Water the compost carefully. Many annuals need to be placed in a warm environment such as a propagator or heated greenhouse, but perennials rarely require heat and can be kept outside in a sheltered position. Keep moist until the seeds germinate and then prick out into trays or individual pots. Tender seedlings that have been sheltered should be hardened off in a cold frame before planting out after the threat of frost has passed.

sowing in a pot
Once the seed have been sprinkled in a pot, cover with compost or a fine grit as recommended for the particular plant.

planting in a tray
For a tray, once seedlings have grown they should be pricked out carefully and planted on in individual pots to continue growing.

planting bulbs
As a general guide, make sure the planting hole for a bulb is at least three times as deep as the bulb is tall.

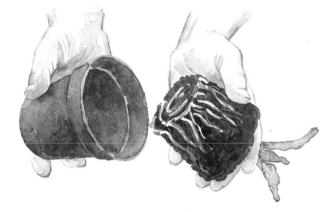

potbound plants
Avoid buying potbound plants such as this.

BULBS

Spring-flowering bulbs are planted in autumn, while summer- and autumn-flowering bulbs are planted in spring. As a rule, the depth of the planting hole should be at least three times the height of the bulb. While daffodils, tulips and several other bulbs can be purchased as dry specimens, it is better to buy many others either 'in the green', that is, freshly dug with their leaves still green, or growing in pots. For example, snowdrops should always be purchased in the green, while cyclamen are best bought as potted specimens. Some plants can be relied upon to increase with little attention being paid to them. These are often naturalized bulbs, those that have been left to grow in grass or under trees. If they become congested after a few years, lift and replant.

BUYING PLANTS

There are several ways of acquiring plants for the border. The simplest is to buy them. Garden centres sell a reasonably wide range but specialist nurseries have a much larger selection, including unusual plants. Many nurseries also sell plants by mail order or online, which is a great advantage if they are some distance away. Order early as demand can outstrip supply for many catalogue plants, and inform the nursery if you expect to be away when the plants are sent, otherwise you might come home to a box of dead plants. When buying plants, do not always go for the largest specimen. A medium-sized plant, free from pests and diseases, is best. Do not buy potbound plants (above).

The alternative to buying plants is to grow your own from seed, by division or from cuttings. This is a much cheaper approach but plants will need time to mature. Rare plants are often only available as seed.

useful addresses

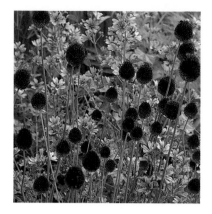

BULBS

Jacques Amand
The Nurseries
Clamp Hill
Stanmore
Middlesex HA7 3JS
020 8420 7110
www.jacquesamand.com

Avon Bulbs
Burnt House Farm
Mid Lambrook
South Petherton
Somerset TA13 5HE
01460 242177
www.avonbulbs.com

De Jager & Sons
The Nurseries
Staplehurst Road
Marden
Kent TN12 9BP
01622 831235
www.dejagerflowerbulbs.co.uk

Rare Plants (Paul Christian)
P.O. Box 468
Wrexham
LL13 9XR
01978 366399
www.rareplants.co.uk

CLIMBING PLANTS

TH Barker & Son
Baines Paddock Nursery
Haverthwaite, Ulverston
Cumbria LA12 8PF
015395 58236
www.ukclematis.co.uk

J Bradshaw & Son
Busheyfield Nursery
Herne, Herne Bay
Kent CT6 7LJ
01227 375415

FOLIAGE AND UNUSUAL PLANTS

The Fern Nursery
Grimsby Road
Binbrook
Lincolnshire LN8 6DH
01472 398092
www.fernnursery.co.uk

Goldbrook Plants (hostas)
Hoxne, Eye
Suffolk IP21 5AN
01379 668770

Halecat Garden Nursery
The Yard
1 Halecat Cottages
Witherslack
Cumbria LA11 6RT
01539 552536
www.halecat.co.uk

Hoecroft Plants (grasses)
Severals Grange
Holt Road
Wood Norton
Dereham
Norfolk NR20 5BL
01362 684206
www.hoecroft.co.uk

The Scottish Bamboo Nursery
Middlemuir Farm
Craigievar
Alford
Aberdeenshire AB33 8JS
01975 581316
www.thescottishbamboo
   nursery.co.uk

HERBACEOUS PERENNIALS

Blooms of Bressingham
Bressingham
Diss
Norfolk IP22 2AB
01379 688 585
www.bloomsof
   bressingham.co.uk

Bridgemere Garden World
Bridgemere
Nantwich
Cheshire CW5 7QB
01270 521100

Cally Gardens
Gatehouse of Fleet
Castle Douglas
Scotland DG7 2DJ
Information: 01557 815029
www.callygardens.co.uk

Four Seasons Perennials
Forncett St. Mary
Norwich
Norfolk NR16 IJT
01508 488344
www.fsperennials.co.uk

Glebe Cottage Plants
Pixie Lane
Warkleigh, Umberleigh
Devon EX37 9DH

Green Farm Plants
Bury Court
Bentley, Farnham
Surrey GU10 5LZ
01420 23202

Hadspen Garden & Nursery
Castle Cary
Somerset BA7 7NG
01749 813707
www.hadspengarden.
   freeserve.co.uk

Langthorns Plantery
High Cross Lane West
Little Canfield, Dunmow
Essex CM6 1TD
01371 872611

Merriments Gardens
Hawkhurst Road
Hurst Green
East Sussex TN19 7RA
01580 860666
www.merriments.co.uk

PLANTS FOR DRY AREAS

Beth Chatto Gardens
Elmstead Market
Colchester
Essex CO7 7DB
01206 822007
www.bethchatto.co.uk

ROCK GARDEN PLANTS AND ALPINES

Inshriach Alpine Nursery
Aviemore
Inverness-shire PH22 1QS
01540 651287
www.kincraig.com

Holden Clough Nursery
Holden
Bolton-by-Bowland
Clitheroe
Lancashire BB7 4PF
01200 447615
www.holdencloughnursery.com

Ingwersen
Birch Farm Nursery
Gravetye
East Grinstead
West Sussex RH19 4LE
01342 810236
www.ingwersen.co.uk

Pottertons Nursery
Moortown Road
Nettleton
Caistor
Lincolnshire LN7 6HX
01472 851714
www.pottertons.co.uk

ROSES

David Austin Roses
Bowling Green Lane
Albrighton
Wolverhampton
West Midlands WV7 3HB
01902 376376
www.davidaustinroses.com

Peter Beales Roses
London Road
Attleborough
Norfolk NR17 1AY
01953 454707
www.classicroses.co.uk

SEED SUPPLIERS

Chiltern Seeds
Bortree Stile
Ulverston
Cumbria LA12 7PB
01229 581137
www.chilternseeds.co.uk

Suttons Seeds
Woodview Road
Paignton
Devon TQ4 7NG
0870 2202899
www.suttons-seeds.co.uk

Thompson & Morgan
Poplar Lane
Ipswich
Suffolk IP8 3BU
01473 588821
www.thompson-morgan.com

Unwins Seeds
Telephone 01244 882555 for
your nearest stockist.
www.unwins-seeds.co.uk

TREES AND SHRUBS

Architectural Plants
Cooks Farm
Nuthurst
Horsham
West Sussex RH13 6LH
01403 891772

Notcutts Garden Centres
Woodbridge
Suffolk IP12 4AF
01394 383344
www.notcutts.co.uk

Spinners Garden
Boldre
Lymington
Hampshire SO41 5PG
01590 673347

Starborough Nursery
Starborough Road
Marsh Green
Edenbridge
Kent TN8 5RB
01732 865614

WATER PLANTS

Mickfield Watergarden Centre
Mickfield
Stowmarket
Suffolk IP14 5LP
01449 711336
www.watergardenshop.co.uk

Stapeley Water Gardens
London Road
Stapeley
Nantwich
Cheshire CW5 7LH
01270 623868
www.stapeleywg.com

credits

The publishers would like to thank the following illustrators for their contributions to the book: Elizabeth Pepperell, Martine Collings, Tracy Fennell, Valerie Hill, Stephen Hird, Sarah Kensington, Amanda Patton, Lizzie Sanders, Helen Smythe and Ann Winterbotham.

They would also like to thank the owners of the following gardens for their help: Axletree Garden and Nursery, Peasmarsh, East Sussex; Bates Green, Arlington, East Sussex; Beth Chatto Gardens, Elmstead Market, Essex; Hailsham Grange, Hailsham, East Sussex; King John's Lodge, Etchingham, East Sussex; Merriments Garden, Hurst Green, East Sussex; Queen Anne's, Goudhurst, Kent; Rogers Rough, Kilndown, Kent; Upper Mill Cottage, Lodse, Kent; Hadspen Garden and Nursery, Castle Cary, Somerset; Cinque Cottage, Ticehurst, East Sussex; Sticky Wicket Garden, Buckland Newton, Dorset; Snape Cottage, Chaffeymoor, Dorset; Grace Barrand Design Centre, Nutfield, Surrey; Holkham Hall Garden Centre, Holkham, Norfolk; Wyland Wood, Robertsbridge, East Sussex; Long Barn, Kent; and Hatfield House, Hertfordshire.

The photographs in this book were taken by Stephen Robson except for the following, which are courtesy of Jerry Harpur: (t = top, b = bottom, c = centre, l = left, r = right) p.34 tr, bl, cr, br; p.35 br; p.74 tl; p.75 tl, tr, br; p.104; p.111.

plant index

general index

acknowledgements

The author would like to thank all those involved in bringing this book
into the light of day: Anne Ryland who made the book possible by
commissioning it; Lynn Bryan for editorial work during the early stages
and Sarah Polden who took over and shaped the book into its final form,
as well as giving plenty of encouragement; Stephen Robson, who
manipulated the camera so adroitly; Mark Latter for the hours
he spent on the design and his endless stream of faxes; and
all the illustrators for the delightful artwork.

Thanks also to all the owners of the beautiful gardens who allowed us to
photograph them especially for this book.